RESTORATION

RESTORATION

The Love That Restored

Ashley Mitchell

Dedication

This book is dedicated to the one whom I call Father. The one who has never left me nor forsaken me even in my darkest days. I dedicate this to Him who has restored me and He who plans to restore you as well.

This book is dedicated to me – for today I am free. When I did not have the guidance I craved or the love I longed for still I was pushed. Pushed by the light inside that sustained me. Therefore, this book is dedicated to me, to who I have become and to you and the you, you will grow to be.

Table Of Contents

"Praise the God and Father of our Lord Jesus Christ! He is the father who is compassionate and the one who gives comfort. He comforts us whenever we suffer. That is why whenever other people suffer, we are able to comfort them by using the same comfort we have received from God."
2 Corinthians 1:3-4

CHAPTER ONE

The Thief of Innocence

*T*he living room was simple. Tiled, a single black leather sofa, and a glass door showcasing the nature outside. I recall a much younger version of myself, happily sitting on that sofa, when I was approached by my cousin. He was only a few years older than me, and practically like a brother. I loved him very dearly, and assumed he felt the same about me. That particular day, in a seemingly genuine tone, he asked if I wanted to play a game. As any child would, I delightfully said yes. He lured me through the darkened hallway into his bedroom. Quietly, I was taken to the top bunk where he slept, and instead of the game I anticipated, he molested me. Eventually, his grandmother came in. Because my underwear had fallen to the floor, she scorned me. I felt the heat of shame burn my cheeks and waited for him to be addressed as well. Rather than admonishing his abusive game, she ignored it and shooed me out of the room.

There, in that home, living in those circumstances, I remained. My father had been in jail, thus forcing me to live there for another month, during which I shared a room with my cousin. On the floor were quilts and pillows, where I attempted to sleep but was interrupted to engage in his nightly game. After a few days, it stopped feeling like a game and felt more like force. I cried as he played but didn't have the courage to tell him to stop. Each night, another piece of me was stolen. I began to feel dehumanized by his lust. I lost all sense of the joyful innocence I once had. The light in my eyes vanished and my smile slowly evaporated. I was left numb.

A month or so later, my dad returned home, and the truth was out. My voice refused to rescue me. But my brother, who knew what was going on, saved me. He courageously told my parents. Though fear arose in my little body, peace eventually settled in, because the storm was coming to an end. I thought I would never see him again, and for that I was grateful. But I was wrong.

To paint the following scene, it was the day before my birthday. I sat on an old wooden chair near the laundry room as my grandmother stood braiding my hair. The peace that hung in the atmosphere was disrupted by a commotion in the garage. I was intrigued by the noise and though my grandmother tried to keep me put, I was able to escape her grasp and investigate. As I tip-toed into the garage, my eyes fell upon the most gruesome sight my young eyes had ever seen.

My cousin, the perpetrator, bloodied, in the clutches of my fuming father. I stood in paralyzing fear, anticipating my own beating. I watched as my father released his anger in each punch. I listened to his screams of anguish and the echoing cries of both of our mother. I stood there watching this unfold in slow motion; my heart raced and my tears were uncontrollable. It all seemed so unreal. I clung to my mother, as we cried in unison. I felt my little body trembling as I waited for it to end – waited for my punishment.

With each blow, my dad grew more violent. He was dragged from my cousin and begged to stop, an instruction in which he complied. Tension finally began to dissipate as my cousin and his mother departed.

To my surprise, as well as my relief, I was left unscratched. I truly thought the incident was as much my fault as it was his. I had told him yes. However, my parents didn't see it that way. There wasn't much conversation about what happened afterwards, but I simply knew that they didn't put any blame on me for the abuse.

Thanks to the innocence of my mind, I repressed the event for years, until I learned more about sexual abuse. However, it was as though the traumatic events were just the beginning for me and my family.

In the days between the abuse and the day I gained a more complete knowledge of it, I watched my family crumble.

CHAPTER TWO

Home of the Fatherless

I come from a family of seven. I'm the second oldest of five, all of whom are boys. As children, my brothers and I lacked nothing. We were extremely spoiled. I would say that we lived a rather lavish life. We had all that we could we desire, except for one thing: the consistent presence of our father.

He was the provider of the family, so he was constantly away on a business venture. He was a car salesman for Toyota; he'd humbly add that he was also the best in the country. As any would which such great achievements, he prided himself in his work. But his work came with a cost, as he rarely had moments of relaxation. He was the epitome of "always on the go."

As a young child, I don't remember seeing him all too much, except when it was to take me on daddy-daughter dates or on family vacations. But because those times were so enjoyable, I don't think I really acknowledged the ramifications of his absence. It was in the midst of his absence that he found himself once again after leaving that lifestyle, tangled in a web of illegalities which ultimately cost him his freedom and family for nearly a decade.

The night prior to the arrest, I had a dream, one I can still vividly remember.

A green hue hung dreadfully in the atmosphere of our home. Men, large and intimidating, welcomed themselves in and began rampaging through our belongings. They inspected every square inch of the house, adamantly searching to discover some sort of mysterious item stashed in our home.

When I awoke, I didn't understand the dream, but I found it to be extremely disturbing. Shaken up and unable to fall back asleep, I left my room and crawled into bed with my mother, who caressed my hair, and assured me that everything was okay. Within minutes, cuddled in the warmth of her arms, I was drifting back to sleep.

After some hours, loud thunderous knocking woke my mother and I out of our peaceful sleep. She made herself presentable and went to see who it was. I peered from the bedroom door having a clear view of her answering the knocking. There, standing in the doorway were two large, intimidating cops.

With little explanation, they welcomed themselves in and rummaged through our home. I cried as I relived my dream. I did not understand what was happening, but because of that event, we lost our home and nearly lost each other. My mother, who was assumed to be affiliated with my father's offense, was also arrested and held for further questioning concerning the charges my father was facing.

My brothers and I were forced to move to another city to stay with different family members, who tried to separate us. They wanted some of us to stay with our family in Jamaica, while the others would stay in the states. My mother was informed about the arrangements being made, and with anguish in her heart, she fought in prayer. Her prayers are what kept us all within minutes of each other; rather than countries apart. When she was released, we were all reunited, but were forced to move in with our grandmother. Her home was small; three bedrooms to be exact. The arrangement could have been done if it was only my mom, brothers, and I, but three other family members had already claimed occupancy. So, there we were, nine people living in a three-bedroom home. 'Cramped' is an understatement.

When my brothers and I discovered this was now our new home, we waited, expecting to see our father as well. Our little bodies raced through the house looking for him. We swore we could hear him do the funny noise he always did to make us laugh. We looked and looked, until we realized he wasn't there, and he wasn't going to be there anytime soon. He was gone. Incarcerated.

I felt defeated, lost, and confused. I felt like I had lost my father entirely. My brothers and I all wailed in anguish. Our cries could have crushed the strongest man's heart. It was the cry of children who were broken. Our lives changed as quickly as it had started. When the move happened, the oldest of us was only eight.

We barely got to experience the fullness of a family. But so it goes. We went our separate ways and settled into our new rooms as we began our new life.

As a six-year-old, it was very difficult for me to cope with my father's absence. I constantly had breakdowns in the middle of my first-grade class. I had them so often, I had to be pulled out during class time in order to regain my composure. There were days I didn't return, but I instead sat in the guidance counselor's office as I explained I simply missed my daddy. He was my whole world and I didn't understand his sudden disappearance. A piece of me was gone, and I simply couldn't hide that.

I was reminded of the void in my heart when other students had their fathers come eat with them during lunch. Seeing them made me seethe with sorrow and jealousy. I didn't know exactly where he was, for the longest I thought that he was in the army, as that is what I was told.

I remember every year on Veteran's Day, my school would put on a play where a soldier – *a father* – would come home to surprise his wife and little girl. Each year, as I watched, I cried a little harder. My classmates stared at me in pity as we walked back to class, listening to the sounds of my sad sniffles. However, everyone had to have been used to the sound of my cries by now, since I rarely went a day without shedding tears.

I suppose I never realized how desperately I needed his love. I wished I had cherished every daddy daughter date, because now, I only had memories to live off of. How I wished to have just one more date, but I'd have to wait years for that day to come.

One night, after school I was having yet another break down. Crying hysterically, my face red and head dizzy. I sunk into my mother's chest as she took me in her arms and brought me to a small family-owned Christian bookstore.

It was one of my favorite places. There, she allowed me to cry outside on a small bench. She didn't speak a word to me, she simply ran her hand over my hair and whispered prayers to the Lord as tears slowly escaped her eyes.

Instantaneously, an angel appeared to us. At least, he was what I perceived to be one. He was an older frail gentleman; his presence alone was comforting. Upon seeing us, he asked my mother if he could bless me. With her approval, he disappeared back into the darkened parking lot to only reemerge with an arm full of teddy bears. Five to be exact, one for me and each of my brothers. Little specks of joy were sprinkled on me, as my tears dried and heartbeat steadied. I was in awe that this man knew teddy bears were my first love. Though I had far too many at the time, these were the most special of my collection.

That man was a true blessing from God. It was the first time I truly felt the embrace and comfort of my heavenly Father, while ironically crying over the absence of my earthly one.

Around that time, I began to pray silently at night and read a small children's bible that I was given. My mother had made church a priority after my father's incarceration. It was something I genuinely enjoyed and looked forward to. It felt natural for me to be in church.

Every Sunday during the altar call, I'd make my way up to give my prayer request concerning the same thing. I went to the same woman each week, Mrs. Sue. She grabbed my hands and smiled, as she already knew my request. My little voice spoke with confidence asking that my daddy would just come home and each week she would pray. Then, before bed, I would pray the same.

Something in me knew prayer worked, so I was excited and expectant. But I was expectant within my own frame of time. Each birthday and holiday, I looked at the door waiting for him to walk in with a ribbon on his head – after all, it was what I prayed constantly for. He would have been my favorite present, but it never happened.

As the years passed, my heart began to grow weary. My belief started to dwindle, but I still persisted with my weekly prayer request.

Eventually, it was revealed that he was actually in prison- not the Army. I was crushed, but upon that realization, doors were opened so my brothers and I could go see him. The process was long and strenuous, but I loved being able to see him, even though it was seldom. The visits didn't last too long, so I held onto every phone call and email that I would get from him. My tears eventually stopped as I adjusted to this new normal. Still, I anticipated his return.

CHAPTER THREE

Recognition

*E*lementary school came to an end, and I transitioned into a whole new world. My father was still not home and the trauma from my abuse began to surface. It wasn't until an educator visited my homeroom class to discuss the different forms of sexual abuse. I sat there listening as she began to shed light on the darkness that I endured. Her description of molestation pierced my heart and sent a fire through my veins. I remember so clearly how my stomach dropped and how fear gripped my neck.

In that moment, I tried to keep my face as expressionless as possible so my classmates wouldn't suspect that she was talking about me. I worryingly scanned the room to see if anyone could hear the thoughts racing through my mind. Thankfully no one was paying attention to me, so I kept my face turned downward. I pretended I wasn't interested in what she was saying, but my ears were tuned in.

The words she said made me sick to my stomach; "incest" and "victim" were the two I particularly remember. My heart sank hearing what I was perceived as. Emotions were triggered within me. I felt anxiety snatch the soundness of my mind. The complete essence of myself vanished.

Once again, the light in my eyes left as my innocence was stolen all over again. I couldn't believe it. I couldn't believe that I didn't remember this event for all of these years.

Immediately following the lecture, kids were back to laughing and joking, but I was numb - frozen. I tried my hardest to mask it, as I didn't want any questions. My classmates socialized, asking one another questions about their little experience with sex. I kept quietly to myself, wanting nothing more than to leave, when a boy approached me.

"Hey Ashley, are you a virgin," he asked, laughing.

I looked at him stunned for a moment, then stuttered, "yea- yes I am."

At that time, I thought that to be molested was also to lose your virginity. I was hurt and disgusted at myself because of the question. In my mind, I was far from pure, much less still a virgin. I hurriedly gathered my belongings and walked out of the classroom.

I'm sure it was just a childish middle school question to him. But to me, it was a shot at my identity. By his question, I felt mocked and afraid. I wasn't sure why it scared me – it just did.

That fear began to grow until it became paralyzing. So much so, I felt the need to protect myself. The fear manifested into my actions. It was from that point on I refused to go anywhere. I was convinced in the deepest part of my heart that if I stepped foot into a place with any boys present, I would be raped or molested again.

I hid myself in my room, only emerging if absolutely necessary. I stopped talking unless spoken to. I didn't want any more attention than normal. I only went places I knew to ensure my safety, but even then, I still anticipated being taken advantage of. This fear caused me to seek isolation from my peers. I had relatively no friends, as I refused to put myself in situations that would cause me to feel afraid.

The fear, mixed with pain, brought forth many anxiety attacks. They became my normal. It was typically small things, or even the mention of sexual abuse that would send me over the edge.

Once, my middle school arranged for my class to go on a field trip to an aquarium. There, at a small souvenir shop, were long stuffed multi-colored snakes, the same kind that my cousin had in his room while he molested me. Upon seeing them, I sharply sucked in my breath and blinked the tears away, containing myself until I could have a moment of privacy.

That night, like many others, I'd crawl into my mom's bed as she'd hush me the same way she did at the Christian bookstore and the night before my father's arrest. She sat there caressing me until my rushing river of tears slowly became like small rain drops. I'd lay there for a moment, head in her lap, as I caught my breath. I'd wipe my face, return to my room, and sleep off my emotional exhaustion.

Though it happened quite often, she never grew weary of being my rock. I didn't have to say a word – I would simply enter her room with tear-filled eyes, and she'd embrace me into her arms. Until I stopped going to her. With each anxiety attack I remained in my room and cried myself to sleep.

I regret no longer going to her. But, it went on for so long, I didn't want her bearing my pain anymore. I was silenced by the thought of being a burden and had no one to talk to about how I felt. It was just my tears, fears, and me.

The fear that I carried was intense. The beginning memories I had with fear began when I was finally old enough to get a job. It was at a small popular fast food restaurant.

During one of my orientations, my manager took me to his office in the back of the restaurant to fill out some electronic forms. He ushered me in and shut the door behind him. As the door closed, my heart dropped and I could no longer hear the words coming out of his mouth. My mind began racing and my stomach turned. Everything in me felt as though this was the moment I'd be yet again taken advantage of.

I held back tears and tried to control my breathing. I felt myself shutting down - producing an anxiety I couldn't control.

He finished his spiel by asking if I understood. Being brought back to reality by his question, I nodded and watched as he walked out the door, leaving me in solitude. The fear I felt in that moment was indescribable, and it was not just on this occasion. I didn't trust anyone, I consistently walked in fear. Essentially, I was the epitome of the feeling. For I knew in the depth of my heart, I would be sexually abused again.

CHAPTER FOUR

The Effect of Confusion

*B*efore the fear fully blossomed, I began to notice thoughts that were seemingly always running through my mind. Thoughts that violently bombarded my peace. Thoughts that pushed me even further into the hands of fear. Thoughts that made me question my sexuality.

These thoughts of homosexuality slowly began to emerge throughout my childhood and adolescence. As a little eight-year-old girl, these thoughts made me curious. I withstood the curiosity for quite some time, assuming it'd dissipate or that it was even normal. However, it persisted, so much so, it turned into an inclination, a desire, even.

I felt something prompting me – pushing me – to research the meaning of the thoughts in my head. After ensuring my privacy, I grabbed a laptop and watched highly explicit music videos. But it wasn't enough. I was still itching with curiosity. I scrolled and searched until I found the closest thing that would satisfy the homosexual thoughts. Watching these videos made me a bit uncomfortable and feel very guilty, because I knew I shouldn't be doing it, but I couldn't help myself. Something in me needed to be satisfied, so I did what I thought was my due diligence. I didn't watch those videos often. Just enough to silence my curiosity, to then went to do what eight-year-olds do. But, the small internet search planted a seed I wouldn't see until middle school, when it truly surfaced and increased steadily from there.

I began to notice the prevalence of these thoughts after learning about molestation. Upon my realization, I became distraught, confused, and extremely uncomfortable. I first remember noticing these thoughts when something provocative aired on TV. A friend of mine loved the show and found it humorous, and she convinced me to watch it with her. At first it was funny, but as the show progressed, the female cast members became rather sensual with one another. I watched in discomfort, and often had to excuse myself to calm down.

I remember my heart racing and stomach turning. I didn't like what I was seeing, but the desires I had were intense and undeniable. I didn't understand how she could sit there and watch the show with no problem, while I felt like I was under attack. It terrified me. I didn't know what was happening or why it was happening, and I certainly didn't know what to label it. But these thoughts were persistent, and the feelings were so prevalent I knew it already had a label. I just couldn't admit it. Even in the midst of my closest friends and family, I kept it hidden. I remained silent out of fear of rejection and hatred.

The volume of these thoughts were loud; excruciatingly loud. I couldn't discern what were my own thoughts. It felt as though my mind was being invaded and taken as a captive. Since I couldn't make these thoughts stop, and the feelings were uncontrollable, I accepted the bondage as my identity. Though it didn't feel natural to claim as my own, I no longer had the strength to fight it. So, it became normal to me. It was just another thing I would be forced to endure. Something I couldn't articulate. Something I couldn't cry about in my mother's arms. Something I had to face alone.

Though I felt being attracted to females was my truth, I didn't want to act upon it. I didn't want people to know, to perceive me any differently, or to condemn me. I masked it. No one knew. I set it up to be that way. My mindset was that if I spoke of it, it'd become more of a reality, and I just couldn't bear it. I didn't want to be associated with it. I truly didn't believe I was a lesbian.

I could never see myself with another female; my desire was to marry a man one day and have his children. But another desire in me lusted after women. The two just didn't align. How could my heart want one thing, but my mind attempt to convince me otherwise? I was confused, and I was petrified. Crippled in fear.

I felt anxiety rise in my chest in social situations with other females. I didn't know how to be their friends; the weight of the shame I felt was too heavy. How could I possibly be friends with someone while harboring such a secret? What if they discovered it? What if I spoke and accidentally revealed it? I took no chances. My aim was to play it as cool as possible. To act "normal". But that normalcy only led to social anxiety and awkwardness. I was too embarrassed of myself and incapable of pretending to be someone else. I got tongue tied, I was intimidated, and ashamed of myself. It was easy to remain in isolation and friendless only because the wall I had built was impenetrable - even for myself.

I did have a few close friends though. I was comfortable being around them as we had known each other for years, but around the rest of my peers it was impossible to be me. It was almost as though I feared being around other girls because I wanted nothing to happen, causing a sense of self-consciousness transpiring into my every movement. I felt like I was constantly doing and saying the wrong things. I feared that my mistakes would draw unwanted attention that would put a spotlight on the secrets I carried.

The only times I felt I was good at upholding the teenage standard was when I was mean. If I was known for anything, it was for that. Although it was merely a defense mechanism, it indeed kept people away, and thus kept my secrets safe. I went to the extent of declining party invitations and refusing to pursue close friendships, because of the fear of my thoughts manifesting into action. Loneliness crushed my spirit, but I desperately sought both physical and mental safety. I had to sacrifice a true social life to protect myself.

As I got older, I became wearier. The thoughts were intensifying, and simply ignoring them no longer sufficed. I felt hopeless. I needed something to alleviate this burden. Around this time, I began to periodically watch porn. It was only ever enough to quiet the thoughts for a bit, to relieve the blistering cravings. Though momentarily, it felt like my only escape, until the yearning intensified again. It was a cycle. Still, I was committed out of determination, to keep it hidden. I dared not to walk in the way my thoughts directed me.

However, despite my will power, the thoughts didn't magically stop. If anything, they became more agonizing, because I starved them from what they truly desired: action. So, there I stood, nearly friendless, fearful, and confused. I feared both men and women and rejected others before they could reject me. I walked around with brokenness but played it off as meanness because I was too afraid to develop relationships. Showing a hard exterior was the only identity I wasn't ashamed of.

Despite my fears of men and developing relationships, I realized having a boyfriend relatively silenced the thoughts of homosexuality. From sporadic flings in middle school to long-term relationships in high school, I was always in a relationship. It was only in the midst of relationships that I, for once, didn't feel a sense of rejection. Since I had these boys to cling to, I needed no other friends. I was treated poorly by every boyfriend that I had. Each used and misused me in their own special way. Luckily for me, however, my mind was redirected to the things regarding my relationship, so much so, that the thoughts of homosexuality began to diminish. However, it was merely a tradeoff; the spirit of homosexuality for the spirit of lust. It was like picking the lesser of two evils, in which I chose lust.

Sex became my scapegoat. As long as I had it, the thoughts were essentially silent. While I was grateful for that escape, the lustful cravings increased significantly. My relationships became consumed by sex; my *mind* was consumed by sex. Growing up, I was no stranger to lust – the molestation opened me up for that. But once I, myself, opened the door to sex, it ran its course in my life, swallowing me whole, digesting every part of identity I had left.

There was a strong part of me that thought it would be nice to wait until marriage. I even took a pledge to remain pure and proudly sported a purity ring during my middle school years. Yet despite my innocent efforts, I caved in when I was sixteen. I needed my boyfriends to want me and shower me with their love. I was desperate for it, and sex was the only way I thought I would get it.

Being in relationships became like a drug I felt incomplete without. They fed into my insecurities, the way they lusted after me made me feel like I was special, loved, and beautiful. I competed for their love with my body, but still always lost. I was just something willing and available for them. I was a playground for their lustful desires. But it felt normal. I thought that this was what relationships were all about. And as far as I can remember, my mind was silent.

So, I became truly consumed by lust and attention. I became desperate for love, so much so, I stayed when I shouldn't have. I knew better, I saw the messages, I knew the infidelities, I sensed their true intentions. Yet, still I stayed, because my heart screamed out in desperation and my body burned to be loved. Why shouldn't I have stayed when I got the thing I truly sought? I had somebody. I wasn't lonely. I felt almost safe in their presence. My mind was at rest, and while it hurt so badly to be in these toxic relationships, the quietness of my mind and the attention was too sweet to leave.

CHAPTER FIVE

A Home Incomplete

*A*t home, my fears and my hard exterior remained, resulting in little communication between my family and I. To be fair though, we hardly spoke to begin with − the silence wasn't anything out of the ordinary. It was as though the hurt and brokenness from all of my family members, myself included, exuded into the atmosphere, separating us to our own corners of the house. I remember a handful of times that we shared laughs and secrets, but pain would rise once again, pushing us apart.

I didn't know how to express my fear or my pain, so I masked it as anger and frustration. I didn't build a relationship with any of my brothers for years because of that reason. To this day, I can hardly engage in "remember when" conversations because the effects of my trauma had bound me to my bedroom for so long.

But in the midst of my own pain, I failed to realize my brothers were hurting too. They too grew up without a dad and endured many things that pierced a hole in their childhood. Yet, I disregarded their hurting hearts and clutched onto my own. Had I averted my attention from my own pain and attempted to communicate with the people who were supposed to be the closest to me, my childhood may have been written differently.

Instead, I took my misplaced pain and hurt them with it. I blocked them out, ignored them, and even blamed one for my molestation. I did it only because I was hurting but not because of him. The truth was, he was the one who protected me.

Regardless of the truth, I was mad because I wanted my father to be the one to save the day, but he wasn't. He made up for his absence during those abusive nights by later defending my honor as he fought the abuser. But my heart wished he was there to prevent it from happening in the first place. His absence in that moment left me feeling rejected - later springing up resentment towards him. I continued to feel rejected by everyone around me, as though to say, "no one else would love or protect me because father didn't". It wasn't until he came home that I recognized those ugly feelings festering in my heart came from him.

He was released from prison my freshman year of high school. I walked through the doors into my living room and saw a man I hadn't fully recognized. He looked differently from what I remembered but I *knew* he was my dad. There he was, *finally*. My brothers and I screamed. We were overjoyed, we laughed as we jumped up and down, fighting over hugs. Things felt complete, but only for an instant.

At that point, we had already moved out of my grandmother's house into a home of our own. We lived with her for a few years. Though from my perspective, there was less hostility in our family, we still endured our fair share of ups and downs. Jamaican slurs were hurled between the adults in the home. My mother's frustration was from my uncle's alcohol and drug use while her children drove with him in the backseat of his car. There was much headache but still my brothers, cousin and I shared laughs and smiles.

 Upon my father's return, our rough patches changed, though only for a bit. We began to have some fun again; I recognized it to be simply the presence of our father that brought us together. But then reality started again, and things shifted.

The fights we all had increased, and awkwardness became a part of the family. I essentially didn't know who my father was. I saw him as just a man who lived in our home. The hurt I once carried as a little girl had grown into bitterness. Anger towards him bubbled up in my being, to the point I couldn't bear holding a full conversation with him. Things felt too far gone. The damage of his absence had been done and the strain on my life felt irreversible.

Up until the point of his return and for years after, I found the need I had for a father in the arms of my boyfriends. One of the reasons I remained in the corruption of the relationships was because of the void left gaping in my heart.

As time progressed from my father's return, life got busy, and the thought of an apology and hopes of even a daddy-daughter date vanished from my mind. The resentment that had surrounded our relationship was one I could not mask – it unashamedly paraded itself all over my face. It was difficult to speak to him or to be corrected by him, but still I tried my best to respect his authority.

Nevertheless, we reconciled by the grace of God. I adjusted my perspective. I recognized my father tried to be a good dad in the best way he knew how; in the only way he was equipped to. So I got over my pain regarding it. I stopped letting the past bother me. we didn't build a relationship but there was no longer a that would spark fire in my bones at the sight of him. I began to forgive, though my forgiveness wouldn't fully manifest until after college.

Eventually he explained to me that his emotional and mental absence as a father in my life came from not wanting to lose me again. He feared that discipling me would push me away. He didn't voice his opinion when he had suspicions about boyfriends I brought over because out of anger I told him that I didn't want his advice. So he stopped telling me what to do and not do. He didn't want me to feel as though he were running my life so he gave me space. To me it was too much space, but to him it was *safe* space.

I cried to him explaining my resentment and that is where clarity, healing and a relationship began. This after college though - at this point, I was still in high school and we were still just living in the same home.

CHAPTER SIX

A Decision to Last

*H*igh school went by quickly. Afternoons were spent with my middle school friend, and weekends were filled with obsessing over my boyfriends.

My family and I still went to church, multiple times a week, but for years, nothing truly stuck to me. My nights were still filled with anxiety attacks and clutching my heart from the pain these boys caused in my life. My insecurities still transcended as I compared myself to other girls on social media and at school. I was still silent, speaking only from places of defensive fear, occasionally pushing myself to laugh and joke with classmates. I became a professional at masking who I was. I portrayed myself as what other people wanted to see and what I perceived to be acceptable, because who I truly was certainly was not.

As my senior year of high school approached, I had been in an on-again, off-again relationship for a year and a half. I had known this boy since I was young, so it was difficult to just walk away. I thought he was my "Adam" or my "Boaz," so I held on tightly to the possibility of a future together. I thought he would be the man of God that I desired. After all, he had read the Bible with me when I asked him to. So, what could possibly go wrong between us?

We were by no means perfect. We frequently had sex but at least we went to church to make up for it. He was toxic to me, wouldn't speak to me for days, but would use a kiss and a date to cover his mistakes. He was trying.

Things began to shift when it came time to submit college applications. I applied to multiple colleges, but only was only accepted into one. It was Christian university in a city I had never heard of. At first, I was hesitant, but as I visited the campus, I fell in love with the atmosphere and felt a sense that this was my home. As the day approached of being an official college student, I grew more and more excited.

Around this time, the homosexual thoughts weren't bothering me as badly as they use to. Though I would have my days, I often triumphed over them. I remember the words of my boyfriend as I discreetly expressed to him how I felt towards females. I left out many details, but confessed it was something I just couldn't help. He said something along the lines of, "If you are already declaring defeat, how will you ever be victorious? You will get past this." Those words encouraged me. I *didn't* have to claim defeat; I *didn't* have to be overcome by this. I *would* be victorious.

It was a turning point, briefly, at least until I got to college. Something in me switched, and it caused me to make the conscious decision to be all that I wanted to be, and to not be bound by fear, lust, or those thoughts. I began to strategize and make deliberate plans to get better. My first step was getting baptized.

My whole life, I was timid in my relationship with God. I believed in Him, but I was never ready to go all in with Him. Then one day, I thought to myself: was I truly a Christian, or was this all a show? Was this for my parent's satisfaction? Had perhaps this just become my norm?

I really pondered on those questions. The last thing I wanted was to go through the motions and never experience God fully. Something in me yearned for Christ. Something in me didn't want to walk away from Him. This Christian life felt right to me. Upon deciding I wanted to dedicate my life to God, I eagerly signed up for baptism.

It was October of 2014 when I made the decision. I was given several sheets of paper to complete, one of which was the public declaration that would be shared while I was being prepared to be dunked under the water. My response wasn't true. I was afraid if I wrote the truth of the things I dealt with, I would be judged. The truth was I was still in bondage. I had yet to give God control over the spirits I dealt with, and I wouldn't for several years.

Nonetheless, something in me was hungry for God. I wanted to be in love with Him like the leaders and pastors of my church were. I wanted to know Him, to know His word, and be transformed. So, I did what I thought was right.

The day of the baptisms, we drove to the beach where it was held. Staring out of the window as my mother drove, I pondered on what my new life would be like. I thought about the fire God was going to place in my heart for Him, and how I wouldn't be able to recognize myself because of my freedom. I was excited and a little nervous, but altogether ready.

The beach was packed with my fellow church members, all wearing the same black baptism shirt. A loud sound booth was set up so the pastor's words would echo throughout the beach. Even families just relaxing and enjoying their Sunday would hear these heartfelt declarations. In that moment, I was grateful my declaration wasn't detailed. It took about half an hour for everything to start. During the downtime, I searched for my boyfriend, hoping I would spot him excitedly waiting in the crowd. I looked for him until my name was called. He didn't come. He chose not to, justifying it by saying it was a special day for me, one that he shouldn't be a part of.

No longer was I anticipating the benefits of my actions. I was grieving over the absence of my boyfriend. I tried to shake him from my mind as the cold water splashed against my legs, but I couldn't. I was hurt. I became distracted. I faintly heard my declaration – "Jesus has delivered me from the pain and lies of this world, He has filled a void in my heart I thought would be there forever with true peace and joy." Then, I was under. I could have stayed there, to really just escape everything for a moment longer. But, my body was jolted back into reality. I forced a smile, and trudged through the waters to be embraced by my family. Still, scanning the crowd. I ruined this opportunity for a boy that didn't deserve me. It crushed me.

However, I now wanted to change my life to walk as a Christian. Despite how I felt, I wanted to do something new with myself. I opened the Word, bought a journal, and began to pray. I did this as often as I could and, truth be told, it felt so good. It felt right, until the attacks came.

I could no longer sleep throughout the night. My bed would shake, waking me to discover my body being pressed down by a heavy force. My breath was trapped in my lungs, only letting the slightest bit of air through. I couldn't move; I just heard and felt--loud footsteps and deep breathing--the sound of things flying above me whilst banging against steel.

I remembered a bible study I went to where the pastor explained to us what sleep paralysis was. I recalled her saying to declare the name of Jesus until He freed us from the weight of the enemy. When those attacks began, I did just that. I pleaded, crying out the name of Jesus with faint whispers, but mainly in my thoughts. After a while, there was a release. I gasped for air, not fully comprehending what had just happened, and stayed awake the rest of the night. Fear struck me on a new level.

I used to say that one of my biggest fears were ghost. I refused to watch anything scary. I couldn't even speak about them. My heart would immediately stop, I'd lose my breath, and feel panicky.

Then came the day when I realized there was a devil and demons. My fear skyrocketed. I had no knowledge on spiritual warfare, I didn't know the enemy didn't want me in my Word and was trying to scare me out of it. I also didn't know the Word was my weapon against him. Every night I would relinquish my authority trying to stay up to avoid the attacks. When in reality God gave me authority over the power of the enemy. God said in His word that I could tread upon snakes and scorpions and crush them without being harmed. (Luke 10:19) Yet night after night I laid in paralyzed fear of being harmed by the hands of the enemy.

Despite the attacks, reading the Word gave me a new sense of conviction. I really wanted to stop having sex. I got serious about it and put little sticky notes on every page that talked about sexual immorality. I still have them there to this day. They encouraged me, and they reinforced what I already knew I should and shouldn't do. But because my boyfriend wanted it, and I wanted to make him happy, it was hard to stop.

My boyfriend going back on his word, not showing up, and not speaking to me for days were normal occurrences. So after the baptism, when he apologized for his absence, I quickly forgave him - wanting to just move on. During that time, I really tried to make our relationship work while being pleasing to God, but my boyfriend was still very adamant about having sex. I, on the other hand, was not. My convictions were too strong. I tried every tactic in the book to make sure I did not have sex with him. I remember him trying to entice me one day, and without a second thought, I put my hands out in front of him and said, "Let's pray". He dropped me home shortly after that. I laugh about it now, and even then I didn't mind. My desire was to grow in my relationship with God, and this boyfriend of mine was giving me plenty of reasons to be single in order to do so.

I eventually began to get really involved in church. I was there three times a week. It became a safe haven for me. My life began to feel brighter. I found a piece of myself I actually liked. She was funny, confident and had a desire for God. Despite who I was and what I knew in my younger years, I felt a slight sense of freedom and the grip of bondage didn't seem so tight.

One night, I was asked to sing on the worship team, which I agreed to do. I knew everyone at the small service, so I wasn't too nervous, but it was my first time doing this, and I wanted my support system there. I looked out in the crowd to spot my boyfriend. He, of course, was nowhere to be found.

This time, I didn't let it hurt me. Instead, I waited on him after service to pick me up and broke up with him. For once, I was happy to be single.

I had nine months before college started, so I focused on graduating high school, being in church, and working a new job I loved. I began to feel true happiness. Something emerged out of the depth of my bondage, and I finally felt comfortable – comfortable enough to speak, to laugh, and to conquer. I felt a sense of newness and I basked in it.

In this time, homosexual thoughts weren't affecting me. I honestly can hardly remember if I even had them. I credit it to being in the Word. The fear was still there, but I wasn't in situations where I felt threatened. For a while, the anxiety didn't attack either. As for the lust, well, I wasn't having sex and I didn't have a boyfriend, per se. I did, consistently however, have boys I "talked" to. Boys who would cater to my need for love and attention while still technically remaining "single"

I thought I had my life under control. I felt good.

CHAPTER SEVEN

A Freshman Story

I entered college with many expectations. I expected the newness and freedom I felt to manifest even more. I expected to continue boldly in singleness. I expected to gain lifelong friends. I expected to develop and utilize a voice of my own.

Initially, I expected much, but gained very little. I was disappointed. My perception of what should have been did not come to pass. Rather than me conquering the ups and downs of college, they triumphed over me. The external factors of my environment controlled who I wanted to be – and I allowed it to. My morality was stripped. Against my better judgement, I was coerced into avoidable situations. College challenged me. It broke me. Ultimately, it would transform me.

It was August of 2015, the beginning of all destruction and growth. I had plans to walk into this new place with an identity that welcomed joy, peace, love, and acceptance. Though internally, I still hadn't truly cultivated those things for myself; I was hungry for a change. The last nine months prior to my freshman year were refreshing. I had developed some confidence, and the bonds that held me back felt rather weak.

I looked at it as a fresh start. No one knew my name, and no one could see my deeply hidden pains. All they could see is what I showed them. So, I showed a girl woven with confidence, boldness, and fun; a girl who was blunt and didn't take foolishness, but also a girl that was kind enough to have friends. The impenetrable wall that was once deeply rooted in the soil of turmoil, I seemingly demolished. I allowed myself to be more open with others, about surface-level things at least. I become a person that others could confide in, that would listen and correct, but always love. I wanted the absolute best for these new friends I made. I wanted their safety, protection, and love to always be guarded.

As for me? I was just a vessel, that drained slowly. I kept everything to myself out of embarrassment. I didn't dare admit when something was going wrong in my life. If I did, it was fixable, and wasn't directly damaging to my reputation. I lived the best of both worlds. I had friends, who trusted and loved me, who wanted to be around me, and would stick up for me. Yet, I still kept my painful truths buried deep, so I couldn't get hurt. It was deep enough that I could forget about my past. This was my new life. This was who I was now. I became okay with that.

My personality differed greatly from the other girls I was religiously around. They were partiers. I, on the other hand, had never been to an actual party, or even a club. They drank every weekend and I mainly refrained from doing so. They eventually understood it was just my personality to not be interested in those things. What they didn't know was the root of restraint was fear. I kept it that way. I allowed myself to be perceived as up-tight, even boring, as some would say, but it didn't bother me as long as my protection was ensured. I didn't care what label I had placed on myself.

Despite our differences, we spent time together daily and our bond became inseparable. We had fun together, laughter was always a common denominator between us. Where one went, we all followed.

We were so close, we began to date a group of boys who were all very close friends and roommates. There was one boy for each of us. Mine in particular tried getting my attention before I took any interest in him. He and my closest friend talked about me constantly. I avoided him for the most part but was spotted during one of our schools welcome week events. He approached me and my disinterest rested heavily on my face. Allegedly he called me beautiful and because I didn't hear him, I didn't respond. To say the least, our first encounter ended badly. But eventually the hostility between us settled, and we exchanged numbers and began to get to know one another. Though I planned on remaining single, the old craving of wanting love stirred up inside me.

We met in August and started dating in October. In the middle of those months, we had already crossed multiple lines. After our first kiss, I told him I wanted him to really pursue me, to show me he was a man of God. I told him it was nonnegotiable, and my purity wouldn't be compromised. I expressed to him my distaste for smoking and partying and how I wanted a deeper relationship with God. He listened. I didn't think he would agree to all of this, and truthfully my hopes were that he wouldn't so that I could have an out. But he did.

He said he wanted to pursue me, assured me that he was a man of God, and promised to keep me out of uncomfortable situations involving weed and parties.

Though he said all of this, his actions did not match. We didn't see eye to eye on what it means to have a relationship with God. Although he never invited me to come, he was still constantly high and partying. And before we even became official, we did every sexual thing but sex itself which came to no surprise. When I told him I wanted to wait until marriage to have sex, he simply said "no promises". He knew what he wanted and I should have known too at that moment. These were none of the characteristics I wanted in a man. Yet, when he asked me to be his girlfriend, I said yes. I was hesitant. The holy spirit placed a sense of urgency in my heart begging me to say no. I wanted to say no, and I *knew* that I should say no, but the word "yes" rolled off of my tongue with ease. Even in the moment I said yes, I regretted the decision.

We were idolized. My friends wanted their boyfriends to treat them the way they thought I was being treated. I couldn't blame them; in public, we were the ideal couple. He acted as though he was truly in love with me. Publicly I loved it, but privately, it was different. With each kiss, he sucked the life out of me. He drained me of my individuality and replaced it with the toxicity of his love. Who he was became my identity. I was transformed into the epitome of his being. I no longer had a sense of Ashley. Rather, I was simply his girlfriend, hidden beneath his shadow, complying to his every desire without complaint or protest. My entire soul changed, externally and internally. I wanted to please him in every way I could. Despite my feelings or views on a matter I quieted myself in order for him to have his way, it was my whole objective to make him happy. I wanted to be the perfect girlfriend. The way I carried myself began to adjust, my speech started to change, even my standards diminished. It was humiliating, but a sense of obligation persuaded me to stay.

It was heartbreaking, but I didn't tell anyone about the truth behind closed doors. How could I explain how this man who everyone deemed as perfect made me feel unappreciated and worthless? How could I explain the dates we went on only resulted from me begging him to take me out? How could I explain how I paid his way for everything, bought him whatever he wanted asked for or not, in hopes of getting at least love and appreciation in return? How could I explain how I felt like I was being used to fulfill his sexual desires?

The perception was that he was the model boyfriend, and I was one of the luckiest girls in school. Instead of exposing the truth, I acted as though those perceptions about our relationship was true. I buried my feelings and held my tongue to maintain this reputation, but to also save me from embarrassment. To admit these things to the people who held such high expectations for us felt impossible. I was glorified for having such an outstanding man. The pedestal we were placed upon was so high, coming down seemed hopeless.

So, I remained with him. My excuse was that I saw potential in him. It was the truth; he could have been amazing. Rather than throwing in the towel, I waited. I figured that after a few months' things would change, so I kept waiting. I told myself if they didn't change I'd leave, but I kept waiting. Eventually, those few months of waiting turned into a few years. Two and a half, to be exact.

In one of my first psychology courses, my favorite professor was recommending a book for the class to read. She was very adamant about us reading the book; she claimed that it was life changing, even *lifesaving*. The book was about potential. Her warning to the class was to **never** date on potential. She said to us all who were currently dating that if we read the book and realized we were dating on potential; she would give us extra credit if we ended the relationship. Nervous laughter filled the room, but she was serious. I knew she was; I felt it in my spirit as her words began to resonate with me. I believe the Holy Spirit told me to read it, but I ignored it. I knew if I did, it would tell me to end the relationship, but I didn't have the strength to leave him. He needed me. He was hurting. Every night he would cry to me about the pain he was facing. He was distraught and seemingly depressed. His stress and anxiety were causing him to become physically sick. He worried me, so I carried all of his burdens to alleviate his agony. Doing so drained me; the weight of his problems combined with mine was crushing. I became an open cavity to be filled with his issues. Because I was never given the opportunity to empty myself, I wore myself thin. It was only ever solely about him. So, I swallowed my issues because he needed me; I vowed to be there for him. It was my expectation that after we worked through his problems, his potential would become his reality. I waited and consoled him with compassion and a smile. I thought perhaps it would speed the process up a bit. Instead, it set the stage for my kindness to be taken advantage of.

Up until this point, the lust was relatively controlled. However, the longer I was in this relationship, it began to intensify. It became imprisoning. I felt obligated to succumb to his lust. I desperately didn't want to do anything remotely sexual. Every time we did, I would cry and he said we would stop. But the next day, his vow turned into pleading, which would lure me in. I saw he craved it. He was thirsty to be pleased and I felt like I couldn't say no. I knew he was used to getting sex when he wanted it, and I suppose I was expected to succumb to him the same. If I dared to refuse, he'd put a pillow in between us and express how he felt like he couldn't even cuddle with me if I couldn't touch him. It was a constant guilt trip. It was selfish and domineering. It was only about him. Knowing it bruised my ego and made me feel like nothing more than a playground for his sexual desires. Yet, I couldn't stop. Otherwise, what would be left of our relationship?

One night, thoughts of the molestation weighed heavily on my mind. I began to weep and realized there were broken pieces that were still piercing my heart. I realized I was not healed, and no matter how much I tried to suppress it, I was deeply still affected by it. The more my boyfriend and I engaged sexually, the more I felt how I did as a child. It wasn't for my own pleasure, but was all for his own gratification. I was distraught. I felt taken advantage of. I felt overlooked, underappreciated, overwhelmed, anxious.

I told him this. I told him I *needed* to stop. I couldn't continue because of my lack of healing. I poured my heart out to him. I stood there with tear-stained cheeks and a flushed face, pleading with him for hours. But nothing changed. After telling him how I felt on the matter, I was back in his bedroom, feeling like I needed to please him. I expressed my feelings to him again, which he responded by saying, "What about me? What about my needs?"

From that moment on, I knew I was fighting a losing battle. I reluctantly dropped all weaponry and surrendered to his yearnings. I continued sneaking into his room, pleasing him sexually, and falling asleep without so much as a hug in return.

Months later, we had sex. and from then on, it was all we knew. Everything was centered around it. Dates *had* to end sexually otherwise it "wasn't a real date". Sorrows *had* to be consoled in sex. Alone-time *had* to have sex incorporated into it. Otherwise, what was the point? We weren't "allowed" to go out of town together unless we were having sex. It was like extra-fine print on a contract I didn't read upon signing.

However, as he would constantly remind me, it was my fault since I was the one who initiated our first time. Each time thereafter, when I'd request that we abstain, the blame was placed unapologetically on me. We'd fuss for a while, but I was ultimately still denied.

There were days I would say no. Those no's would lead into his manipulative pleading. His pleading would lead to me feeling guilty and forced to comply. I'd laid there, mind drifting, with sharp pains shooting at my pelvis as he had his way with me. I didn't want to be there; my body knew it. It would clench up as if to protect myself from the abusive nature of what was happening. But without sex, our relationship would crumble. I knew it would; that's all it consisted of, apart from him pouring his problems out on me, telling me his aspirations, and watching movies. All we did was have sex. That was the depth of who we were as a couple and my heart ached because of it.

But, I found ways to encourage myself through it. I thought, *didn't all relationships struggle? Isn't it a goal to go to hell and back together?* That is what society glorifies and praises so why should we be exempt and have a healthy relationship? So, I endured it, just waiting to come back from hell.

CHAPTER EIGHT

I Wanted to Have You

*T*hroughout the beginning of our relationship, I still maintained a close bond with my group. However, our late-night dorm talks turned into weekend turn-up sessions. While by nature and fear I was not the partying type, I felt compelled to uphold the standard within my group. I still refused to go to the club, but settled on outings to hookah lounges and even the occasional kickback. I stuck close to my friends and boyfriend all night to ensure my safety and fed off of their energy. It was difficult for me to ever get up and dance because I was timid and embarrassed to do so.

Though no one said it, I'm sure frustration arose about how I was the only one in the group who sat still the entire night. I felt as though I had already compromised greatly, but now my character was being tested to see if I could maintain my status-quo. Maybe it was my own thoughts trying to convince me of it, but I wanted to be accepted. I tried to push the partier out of me. However, this sort of push felt impossible. Just out of who I was, I simply couldn't; I was too afraid and too bashful.

Then, something clicked in me – I realized I was too sober. Almost every event, my friends would all come in high and though I was not one to smoke, I didn't mind drinking. I no longer wanted to watch while everyone else had fun while I wasn't going to sit back in fear.

I began to depend on alcohol to bring out the best pasts of me. You know, liquid courage. Whenever, anxiety would rise I would take a sip. This made all the parties and outings doable. Truth be told, I began to enjoy who I was in that state as well. I knew my limit, and only drank what I needed in order to do what needed to be done.

The next day, I would just need to rejuvenate--get back to a calm state of mind. I needed alone time, but I was surrounded by my friends and boyfriend nonstop. Even when sober, I felt I was always on the go--always forced to keep up with everyone else--always pushing in some way. Between classes, my boyfriend, and friends, I was exerting all of my energy with no source of replenishment.

I'd lost sight of who I was before coming into college; I'd lost sight of who I wanted to be. I was becoming something for everyone else, all the while leaving God out of the equation. I was no longer in the Word, my church life was sparse, and my conversations were typically not centered around God. All of my passions for developing a relationship with God had vanished. Once, I even expressed the heaviness in my heart for the Lord, and my boyfriend told me essentially it wasn't as deep as I thought it was. God loved me and it was all I needed. Instead of fighting past the ignorance of which I knew he spoke, I nodded my head in agreement. But I knew that there was a part that I had to play in order to have a relationship with God.

I was consumed by the things college threw at me. I became completely off-balanced. While I desired purity, I remained in lust. I wanted to cultivate joy and peace, but my life embodied drama.

Since I typically strayed away from groups of friends, drama was entirely new to me. The only source of drama I recall was immature middle school mishaps. Now, to be in college and dragged into drama on a weekly basis was ridiculous to me. Some of this drama was centered on boys, others from disagreements between the girls, but all stemmed from pride. The relationships between us girls became unstable. We began to slowly drift apart, even before the year could end.

Altercations, both physical and verbal, started to arise among us. We called each other derogatory slurs and ridiculed each other's insecurities. We ganged up on one another and taunted each other until we walked in false power. Still, somehow, we all remained "friends." Despite the gossiping and the fighting, our dysfunction became a comfortable norm.

For the boys, tension began to rise amongst them as well. Specifically, they began to look at my boyfriend differently and no longer included him in their outings. He and I spent a lot of time together and he even cut back on smoking-something the boys didn't like or agree with. As the end of their friendship loomed on the horizon, distance began separating them all. Some moved off-campus, others dropped out, and one even got kicked out. After multiple disrespectful events, their friendships between my boyfriend and I officially ended.

As freshman year came to a close, I had my boyfriend, and the girls and I were still cordial. It absolutely wasn't the same as it was in the beginning. Still, with tears in our eyes, we embraced one another promising to talk over the summer and hopefully even see each other. We said our I-love-you's and goodbyes and parted ways.

CHAPTER NINE

The Grip of Toxicity

*D*uring that summer, my family and I decided it would be beneficial for me to move off-campus into an apartment. Doing so would lower the cost I paid for tuition, as room and board would no longer be a factor. I was ecstatic. I originally wanted to be off-campus, but was unable to, according to the rules my university held. Now was my chance to experience a true taste of freedom. Since the cost of living by myself was too expensive at the time, I asked my closest friend from back home to move in with me. Excited to leave her parent's house, she said yes. After much searching, and with our parent's approval, we found a cute, spacious, two-bedroom apartment and secured the move-in date as quickly as possible. In August of 2016, we moved in.

It was such a dream. Though the apartment did have its various problems, we loved it. Living with each other was fairly easy. She and I had gotten along together very well. Much of our similarities and struggles complemented one another, so we were able to create a rather peaceful environment.

Meanwhile, my friends from freshman year also moved off-campus, ironically into the same complex. Initially we made the effort to see one another, however the occurrence became a rarity. Instead, our friendship consisted of brief encounters on campus and an extremely rowdy group chat.

Though we were rarely in each other's presence, problems began to surface once more. I made a conscious decision to take a step back, and everyone else began to drift away as well. Some went rather abruptly, while others took more time to release. Ultimately, those who I began my college career with became nothing more than familiar faces attached to memories.

Though my boyfriend and I decided against living together before marriage, my apartment somehow became his dwelling space. My room was besieged with his belongings. My closet became the holding cell for his shoes and clothes. I was suffocated by his presence. Yet, I sat in silent compliance, watching as my space was invaded.

When his company became overbearing, I made the bold choice to confront the issue. I empathetically expressed to him my need for space. By the look in his eyes and the pout on his lips, I knew he didn't want to leave, I stood my ground momentarily but eventually gave in, allowing him to come and go as he pleased. He called me almost every night around 3 am with desires to come spend the night. I, having to be up in a few hours, reluctantly agreed. Every time he would come over, he'd be in tears, expressing his fear of failure and ending the night in some sort of sexual act. I was tired, to say the least. I felt like I was in this relationship all on my own, carrying weight I could not adequately bear. He ate all of the food and used all of our toiletries; I asked him to help replenish what he used, to which he replied, "get a job." I was his source of income, his safe place, and his unloading ground of every mental, emotional, and sexual thing.

Up until this point, my spiritual life was rather shallow. My heart still yearned for God, but my actions didn't show it. Though it was internal, it was my desire to be encompassed by the presence of the living God. External things disrupted and hindered it from becoming a reality. My faith had withered into dust, and all that remained were ashes from a fire once lit inside of me.

My joy and peace became carnal, dependent upon earthly forces. I was swayed every which way, with my 'yes' meaning 'no' and my 'no' meaning 'yes'. My mind paralleled the man in the book of James, who was described to be double-minded. I claimed to want a flourishing relationship with God, but my faith was nourished in the soil of instability. The two lacked correlation.

My prayers were without depth and filled with empty words. I prayed as though I was talking to a God too far to hear the quietness of my voice and the ambiguity of my request. I stepped into a world of rituals for the religious and abandoned the desire for transparency within our relationship. The strength I held became my source, and though it was able to sustain me momentarily, I would experience a new level of exhaustion soon after. I suppose it was why Hannah prayed 1 Samuel 2:9: "For a man does not prevail by his own strength."

If I had known it then, I would have emptied my hands of all the futile things I so willingly carried. How the posture of my heart would have shifted if I allowed the vulnerability of my soul to transcend into my prayers. How much heartache I would have avoided. Yet, I was unaware. I thought through Christ I could do all things, even though the things I did were outside of His will. The things He was prompting me not to do. I thought I could still endure and prevail through it all.

Imagine my surprise when my world began to crumble.

The longer I stayed in this relationship and neglected developing one with the Lord, my hopes of true love and freedom blew through my fingers, as sand does in the wind. Even then, in the midst of my foolish ways, Jesus wanted to be the light of *my* world. But I was far too consumed with the exaltation of others to give Him a second thought. Yet, still He patiently and lovingly waited. Though my prayers lacked specificity, God knew the thoughts I kept harbored in my heart. He had placed a desire for Him in the depth of my being but the only way I would walk in the manifestation of it was if I were single.

Yet, embracing singlehood was not something I could simply do. Our souls had been knitted so closely together, I didn't have the clarity I needed to recognize this love was a counterfeit. Still, God placed a gentle sense of knowing inside of my heart. This knowing told me I was in the wrong relationship. It whispered to me, "things aren't going to change, but my child, I have better for you."

Even though I knew I was in the wrong relationship, I failed to leave. My sense of obligation was too powerful to release this relationship I had committed all of my effort to. God knew it, so He opened a door for me. A door of escape. A door in which I could have exited from, locked and abandoned for my safety, my sanity, and deliverance.

With our relationship approaching the one-year mark, I still ignorantly hoped for his potential to bloom into reality. I thought after we crossed this milestone, he would finally, *truly* be in love with me.

Yet, I was wrong. The manipulation got worse, and I was still being taken advantage of. It was disclosed to me, he had intentions to cheat on me.

After an incident on our first anniversary, his form of revenge was infidelity. My expectations of a promise ring were devastated as I was presented with two oversized rings of plastic-like material. The heaviness on my heart and disappointment in my chest were evident. My self-worth diminished and I saw that through his eyes I was valued very little.

Hurt by the expression on my face, he built a wall of animosity and strife between us. His anger boiled towards me as he devised his plan of action. Upon being told of his schemes by his best friend, everything in me shattered. It would be hours before I would see him next and I made the decision to end the relationship.

When the time came however, I lost all courage. He cried as I yelled, and I cried as my heart broke. He dropped to the floor, asking if I was going to leave him. I got quiet. Wanting to say yes, literally seeing my door to get out. Yet, I still answered with a weak, "I don't know."

That night, we got high together for the first time. It was supposed to calm me down and help us communicate better. He became seemingly honest with me and told me the mindset he held throughout the year. Just as I suspected, he did have a problem paying for things, resulting in dates and gifts on my tab. He also told me he had not been giving me the fullness of his heart, but made a declaration, saying those days were behind us.

With belief and hope beaming in my heart, I forgave him. The door I had so longingly anticipated was shut, bolting us in for nearly two more years to come.

CHAPTER TEN

The Rise of Trauma

*I*n the first few months of 2017, the newness I briefly felt was dismantled. What I thought was freedom from the bondages that once haunted me turned out to be a façade. I became proficient in ensuring these strongholds didn't blossom into their full capacity. They were hushed, as I was absorbed by sex and consumed with the vanity of life. In my spirit, I knew that they still lingered, but they were no longer my adversaries; rather, my comfort with them made them my companions.

It was not until I was in a thought-provoking psychology course when I realized the cold, heavy chains of bondage were wrapped around my neck. It was a vulnerable and tender moment in class, as a majority of the girls voiced their background with sexual abuse. The room was drenched in painful, broken tears as heaviness rested upon all of our shoulders. We commiserated with one another, all crying in sympathy.

Finally, it was my turn to speak.

Instead of words, wails of anguish escaped my mouth. I attempted to explain my childhood but was too choked up to do so. The only discernable words to escape my lips were "I'm not healed."

Unable to gain my composure, I excused myself to the restroom, where I wept defenselessly on the floor. Fear and resentment burned in my heart. I felt captured once again. This time, the intensity was stronger. Fear breathed down my neck, and reminded me I would soon be raped, so I'd better get prepared.

Worthlessness and insecurities threatened to suffocate me. Fierce anxiety manifested and partnered with an inability to articulate the pain that resided deep within. A cloak of hopelessness drooped over my shoulders as I, red-eyed and puffy-faced, returned to class in defeat.

As I began to unearth the severity of my pain, my body started to shut down. The trauma was too intense, it seemingly forced my body to abstain from sex. I could longer be the girl my boyfriend longed for. The thought of sex terrified me. Depression tied my hands and feet and duct taped my mouth. I felt defenseless. All I could do was float in the pool of my tears.

I was not eating well, or drinking enough water. I wasn't taking care of myself, and I began to have intense stomach pains that drove me to the doctor's office. Since I was already there, I was prompted to take an anxiety evaluation, which I scored relatively high in. This led the doctor to recommend me to take medication.

Appalled by the recommendation, I refused. I wanted to be in control of my mind, and I didn't want any assistance in doing so.

While in the doctor's office, I was urged to take an STD test as well. The doctor explained to me that it was free, and it is beneficial for everyone to take one routinely. Though reluctant, I agreed, certain everything would come back negative.

In the following weeks, I went back to the doctor's office for a follow up. As I sat in anticipation awaiting my results, she slowly entered the room and regretfully informed me that I had chlamydia.

I tilted my head to the side and scrunched my face as shock, frustration, and confusion crashed over me.

I immediately blamed myself for not being more careful when I was younger. I assumed this virus had lived in my body for years. Not for a second did I question the loyalty of my boyfriend. I couldn't fathom the thought of him cheating on me, especially not while I was in the midst of all of my pain. I refused to believe it.

That night, I told him what the doctor said; if I had it, he did as well. He sat across from me as I blurted out the prognosis. A thick bed of silence fell in between us. His eyes blanked. After a few seconds, I timidly rose and left him alone in the room with his thoughts, knowing there'd be no effective communication. After some time, I returned. He questioned my loyalty, to which I assured him of my faithfulness.

Within the following days, I took him to be tested and treated. My mind was clouded as we drove. Ripples of silence pierced through the entire car. With my eyes straight and focused on the road, my grip began to tighten around the steering wheel. My knuckles whitened as I used my nails to press into the foam. My breath quickened and tears slowly trickled from my eyes. I felt my chest begin to tighten and the tears turned into a rushing waterfall. My boyfriend worryingly looked over and told me to pull over.

As I pulled into the parking lot of a small church, I began to scream, kick and punch, bloodying my knuckles and bruising my shins. We traded seats, and I cried in the passenger's seat until the wave of anxiety passed as my boyfriend drove to his appointment.

I couldn't speak, I couldn't explain it; all I knew was the weight of the world sat on my chest. Ribs snapped and my heart dulled its rhythm. With each passing second, I withered away with no hope of solace. I was consumed with thoughts of the abuse, and was now filled with guilt over an unexplained STD.

As a psychology student, I was not foreign to the concept of counseling, but I was extremely skeptical. After several failed attempts with therapy, I set up meetings with a professor, who recommended a book to me. *The Courage to Heal: A Guide for Women Survivors of Sexual Abuse.* As I read, my brokenness became even more evident. Tears escaped my eyes, blurring my vision as I read. The root of my fear was confirmed, as were many other toxic characteristics I embodied. Like why I felt incapable to say no or to set boundaries or why I felt like my worth was strictly sexual. This book was a reminder that I was not a victim a survivor. It also told me I could heal. All I wanted was to heal. To walk in peace, without the anticipation of fear.

Yet, it seemed unattainable.

In that moment I felt bitter towards the book. Reading it was not going to change my past, nor the facts of it. And I certainly doubted that it was going to mend the broken pieces I carried.

I needed action.

I couldn't be passive in the process of finding healing. I needed to move. I asked my professor what she thought would be an appropriate plan of action as I expressed to her my worries.

I told her I didn't like the counseling, and my doctor wanted to put me on medication.

I told her I replaced my apprehensions with violence. When I was threatened with an anxiety attack, I would begin to hit things until the skin on my knuckles was raw.

I told her I walked in anticipation of being sexually abused, and she couldn't convince me otherwise.

I told her I was tired. Tired of being bound.

I was furious, too. Furious that after years, I was still affected by someone else's actions.

I couldn't take it anymore. I refused to.

Her response: "be careful," and to proceed with caution. I planned on confronting my abuser, but there was no stopping me. In my heart of hearts, I believed this was the right thing to do. I saw no other escape from this mental and emotional captivity but this one. So, the search began.

Uneasiness and dread consumed me. I searched with doubt and fear entangling my thoughts. Still, determination drove my actions to completion.

As I probed through profiles on social media, I became weary. All I knew was his first name, so I had to go to someone who could further assist me: my father. At this point, our relationship was not solidified, but I knew that if I had an issue, I could turn to him.

I still had a piece of resentment towards him, as I still hadn't gotten an apology. An apology for leaving me in a situation that caused seemingly permanent damage. Maybe it was all just too painful for him to address. Nonetheless, I felt a sense of injustice placed upon me, which prevented our relationship from flourishing.

When I called him and told him my intentions, the line was silent for a moment. I had struck a nerve in his heart he'd tried to keep concealed.

"Ash," he said apologetically, "I'm sorry, I didn't know you remembered that. You were so young. I blamed myself for that for years-"

As the conversation progressed, my heart softened. The genuine remorse in his voice touched me. Though he was pained to do so, he gave me the full name of my cousin and his family members. He gave me warnings and precautions, but blessed me to receive healing. That was a major turning point in my relationship with my father, which would gradually improve over time.

Now, with a new peace, and vital sources of information, the search began again.

Within days, I found him and most of his family members on Facebook. His image haunted me; he looked nothing like what I remembered, but I knew he was the one.

He did not use Facebook very often, so my messages were left unread for days. I grew anxious, and decided to message a cousin of his. I told him we were family, and that it was crucial that I get in touch with him as soon as possible. Fortunately, he saw the message, and within 48 hours, he kindly responded with my cousin's phone number.

I sat in my car, staring at the number on my screen. Fear threatened to overpower me, but I had come this far. I had to follow through with the plan.

I held my breath as I texted his number.

I began by introducing myself as his cousin, then questioned if I could call him later in the day. I refused to do this over text, but I certainly couldn't do it in person; I decided a phone call would suffice. As I hit send, my heart thudded in my chest, hard enough to disintegrate every bone in my body. I took deep breaths to control my anxiety, in an attempt to mentally and emotionally stabilize myself.

As the day went on, I waited in fearful anticipation. I paid very little attention to my classes, as I was checking my phone constantly.

It was towards the end of my school day when I finally received a response.

His excitement sickened me. He expressed how he missed my family and I, and looked forward to our conversation. His response confused me, but my professor warned me the probability of denial would be very likely. I took that into account, and dialed the number.

"Cuz!" he exclaimed.

I got straight to the point.

"When we were children you molested me."

I proceeded to tell him what he did to me, and what he made me do to him. I expressed the damage it caused and the fear it provoked within my daily life.

Initially, he was in disbelief, denying such a thing happened, and claimed the extent of any sexual occurrence between us only entailed kissing.

I refused to have my pain discredited.

"No, that's not the story-" I persisted. After much discussion on the matter, he apologized. Shame filled his voice as he sought forgiveness. The conversation continued for a bit longer, and I forgave him. I removed the disgust I once felt and exchanged it for closure.

I ended the call with a sigh of relief. I felt as though something had shifted. Was I healed? No, not even close; only the Lord could offer me complete restoration. Through forgiveness, however, I felt a sense of freedom from the bondage of abuse.

I felt the chains of victimhood loosen its grip on me. I felt God wanting me to draw nearer to Him, wanting the whole of me. He was pushing me in the direction to now pursue Him. It was as if He was slowly directing my path, realigning my heart towards Him.

But I didn't recognize it. I was still consumed with the STD ordeal.

After the conversation with my cousin, I spoke to my professor again, who advised me to seek counseling once more, and to take steps toward recovery. So, I did. I began going to a victim's services agency in hopes of fully releasing my trauma.

I was sitting outside, preparing myself to go into my first session, when my phone rang.

It was my boyfriend with news that confused me, but also relieved me. The results of his STD testing were in, but they were negative. He spoke in a voice of surprise and proceeded to convince me that I, too, never had it, and that we had nothing to worry about. Naively, I believed him. I hung up the phone and began my short counseling journey.

Counseling didn't last long at all; I assumed I had healed and sought no other help. I didn't fear being sexually abused as much, and the anxiety concerning the molestation subsided. The thoughts of the STD left my mind for months. I didn't really focus on it. I became too consumed with other things, such as discovering my identity and cultivating my purpose. However, I did these things in my own strength, leaving me empty once again.

CHAPTER ELEVEN

Who I Have Become

*I*n this new season, I assumed that if I simply found my purpose and cultivated my passions, I would be rewarded with the happiness I'd been lacking. I thought a sense of completeness would overwhelm me and I would walk in the manifestation of success. Unfortunately, I did not know my passion, nor did I grasp the fullness of my identity. So, I began to dabble in different things, hoping clarity would come over me.

During that time, my identity was contingent upon who I was in a relationship with at the time, which was my longtime boyfriend. I was told I was *JUST* his girlfriend, and I was nothing more than a shadow of the man I was with. I perceived those words to mean I had nothing to offer the world, and all I'd ever be was background noise. I was hurt – crushed, even – to know someone actually saw me through this perspective. I assumed everyone else did as well.

However, I knew that there was more to me. There had to be.

I became determined to figure it out, to create a platform for my own name, so people could see the true essence of me even if I couldn't even fully see it in myself. I wanted to emerge from the darkness and let the light I thought I had shine.

While yes, those words about my identity hurt, they also motivated me. I became hungrier to discover the depth of myself. I had to realize what I loved, and what I was good at.

Towards the end of my sophomore semester, I decided to adjust my mindset to one of growing my confidence and walking in self-love. Yet, my form of self-love was not conducive to my growth whatsoever. I began to alter my attributes in a way that glorified the approval of others, rather than my own sense of morality. My soul was desperate for approval, to fit in culturally; I figured I would find my true sense of happiness and peace through it.

As the summer began, I was compelled to find a job. It was refreshing to make my own money and find a sense of purpose in my work. I worked at a retail store selling shoes. Working there made me dress up daily, and pushed me beyond my comfort zone by engaging with customers while exuding enthusiasm. This habit stuck with me because it became easier and easier to pretend to be someone I actually liked.

I worked very often, going in at least 4 days a week and for at least seven hours most days. I didn't have time for much else, so when I came home, any activity was fair game. Most of the time, I'd get high with my roommate and her boyfriend.

This was new to me. I was never one to smoke, but I was tired of who I was and wanted to cultivate a sense of newness about me. When I had days off, I would drive for hours on end to another state just to see my boyfriend, only to stay cooped up in his room numbly having sex. My insecurities ran deep, deeper than what I could truly articulate. I felt unworthy and undervalued, so I pushed myself to do things that I saw others doing, thinking it'd fill a void in my heart, but instead it just tore it open even wider.

I was left unfulfilled, and a sense of depression slowly washed over me.

There were days when I contemplated swerving the wheel and ending the frustration and sorrow I endured. It felt as though there was nothing I could do to receive the internal peace I sought.

I looked to my boyfriend to give me acceptance, to simply call me beautiful or make me feel a sense of worth, yet received nothing. Nothing I did was able to grab his attention and provide me with the wholeness I sought. No matter the way I dressed, did my makeup, or changed my hair, I still could not find completeness.

My job didn't satisfy me, and my actions were not fulfilling. Though I walked with a smile plastered on my face, my heart was clenched and throbbing in sorrow. I lived as though I had no faith in the Lord. Inwardly, my heart still wanted to belong to God, but outwardly, I stopped caring. The environment I was in made it too hard to follow God, so rather than trying to change it, I became it.

I grew more numb and more unfulfilled than I already was. Eventually, my skin began to crawl, because the things I indulged in were not me. They didn't represent who I wanted to be, and they certainly didn't satisfy me in any way.

Once the highs wore off and the sex ended, I was still discontent with who I was. If anything, smoking made me feel more anxious, and the sex made me more insecure.

After the failed attempt of drastically changing myself, I decided a change of environment would suffice, so when the appropriate time presented itself, I moved into a one-bedroom apartment.

The change was as refreshing as it was necessary. I felt as though I had a fresh start and would have the opportunity to discover the fullness of myself. The isolation was relaxing. I enjoyed coming home to peace and righteousness. Where it was my rules, and my way alone. Where I could create the environment I wanted. I was grateful.

It being summertime, my boyfriend was home with his family, so we rarely saw one another. I didn't necessarily mind, as it offered me more peace and time to really work on myself in a distraction- and sex-free setting.

Since I was working, I saw it as an opportunity to take a break from the solitude. I worked at an upbeat shoe store. My manager, coworkers, and I were always having fun and making the most out of our day.

When a photographer came in, we of course took it as an opportunity to have a tiny photoshoot in the store. Immediately, the photographer and I clicked. She thought I was good at modeling, and asked if she and I could continue to shoot together. Excitedly, I agreed.

The pictures made me feel beautiful, and the hype I was given made me feel validated, yet my heart didn't beat for modeling. However, since I felt as though I was incapable of doing much else, I genuinely considered her proposal of working together.

Within a week or two, I agreed, and she and I began to shoot. After our first shoot, we went to a restaurant for dinner and we began to share more of our passions and backgrounds. I told her I wanted to be an author one day, and she challenged me to begin writing. To publish something, *anything*.

She was encouraging and very influential, and I was enticed by her words to simply *do*. My confidence was low, and I still thought other things would be better to invest in. She and I never met again after that, and my modeling journey died as quickly as it began, but her words resonated with me for months. They prompted me to consider taking action on what still lingered in my heart and I had attempted to bury.

Within a few months, as the summer came to an end, I was back to writing.

I loved writing. I have loved it since I was a little girl, making makeshift novels, and spending nights swapping written stories with a family friend.

But then, for years, I downplayed it and even neglected my talent. I wrote only poems when I felt good by the boys I was in relationships with. Other than those instances, I only used my skills to get good grades on school papers. Even then, I didn't write to my fullest potential.

As the fall semester began and I realized my untapped potential, I began to write. I was encouraged by a friend of my boyfriend's to create a blog, one to encourage and empower women and anyone else willing to read. This had not been my first blog, but it was the first blog I had actually cared for. I poured myself out in a way I never would have imagined I would. I became authentic and vulnerable sharing bits of my story and small parts of what I was currently enduring.

I shared to a limit. I was fearful of sharing the entirety of myself. Still, what I did share was liberating. A piece of my identity was revealed as I wrote. I discovered a small part of the essence of my being as I encouraged, and my heart began to feel lighter as I immersed myself in it. It was as though my spirit wrote for me, showing me glimmers of who I would become.

Writing was freeing for me, but most importantly, it was insightful for others. It touched others in a way I had not expected. Their responses were heartfelt, and it motivated me to continue.

The Lord's hand was all over that blog. Within the first month, I was blown away by the demographic of my readers, and the amount of views I had in such a short period of time. There were people from multiple regions in the world. I quickly surpassed over 500 views.

Yet, at the time, I didn't recognize His fingerprints on it. I began to consume myself with distractions that screamed for my attention, rather than going after the thing I felt called to do and felt fulfilled doing. Shortly after the blog was birthed, I began to neglect the gift God had given me.

The foolishness I had been allowing in my life obstructed my focus and I became inconsistent, then my inconsistencies resulted in me completely stopping. My blogging was lacking something essential – Jesus.

I initially created my blog to glorify me, to point at me, and show people I was significant. Each comment, view, and like validated me and made me feel good about myself. I truly did find fulfillment and purpose in writing each vulnerable post, but I gave no glory back to God.

I blame my blog's end on my lack of intimacy with Christ. I didn't know or acknowledge God the way I should have. Essentially, I disregarded God. Despite my routine prayer and bible reading, there was no real relationship between Him and I. If I had truly sought Him, I would have found the fullness of my passion and purpose hidden in him.

Regardless, I was broken. I had no solace, and I lacked what I so desperately thirsted for. Causing consistency of any good thing to be impossible because I didn't have Jesus, the one thing that was supposed to be the most constant. He who was supposed to empower me to walk in my calling.

I was stuck in trying to please my boyfriend, while I also wanted to uphold and develop this new one I had been tempted to find in Christ. But the two conflicted with one another. It was impossible for the two to flourish at once; something had to give. I couldn't walk in the calling of the Lord while swaddled in the demands of man and the requirements of the world. This is where I encountered the most adversity within myself.

There was a desperation that burned in my heart. My spirit wept, and something in me knew the only thing that could quench this thirst was to develop a relationship with the Lord.

I attempted to seek Him, and as I did so, I felt as though I lacked a vital piece which would cause my relationship with Him to flourish. As I tried to discover the piece, the yearning in my heart gradually increased. I began to seek God in the only way I knew how. I read the Word, but nothing I read became rooted in my heart.

The one thing that always struck me as I read was the call to purity. It truly burdened my heart to stop having sex. It was as if it would be the catalyst for my breakthrough. I sought it, but couldn't seem to obtain it. The crying in my heart for the Lord was excruciating, and became even more so the more I put my relationship over God. I knew I needed to remain pure, I *wanted* to remain pure. Yet, I couldn't stay true to my word because my boyfriend didn't seem to have the same conviction, and the one time that he did suggest stopping, we still found ourselves back in the same lustful predicament.

He and I were involved in a small fast with two other friends. Wanting the Lord to reveal Himself to us, I spent time in prayer and my word.

Hurricane Irma came, and we evacuated the school we attended and went to his family's home to seek shelter. Because of the inconvenience, we put the fast on a pause. There, as the sky darkened outside, my boyfriend and I sat on his bed watching movies. We kissed, and immediately things threatened to escalate, but before they could I was in tears. I couldn't do it – my heart started losing the desire to do anything sexual. The obligation and my own desire I had towards the act began to disintegrate.

As my boyfriend rose to get me tissues to dry my wet eyes and running nose, I heard the voice of the Lord.

I was in awe. I had never heard Him speak in such a clear and audible way before. He spoke to me saying, "Put Me first." That's all He said to me, but the words resonated in my heart.

My boyfriend returned and I dried my eyes. He, too, expressed his convictions, but something about his words didn't feel like the conviction I felt. His words sounded empty – sympathetic, but empty. I nodded at his apology and leaned back awkwardly into his arms.

The thought of putting God first transcended the capacity of my mind.

I didn't even understand what it meant at the time. I had never seen a relationship in which God was first. Nonetheless, I believe it was my sign to go deeper and seek Him more fervently.

As my boyfriend and I resumed our fast, God showed me in-depth dreams of infidelity and what would happen if I stayed in the relationship. I would miss my timing to walk into my destiny because of how obligated I felt to be in this relationship. I would not see my purpose manifested. I wouldn't see salvation in my family and in those connected to me.

If I stayed, I would have never gained a sense of identity.

These dreams came to me in the midst of fasting. It was my first time fasting, and I believe once I moved myself out of my own way, God was giving me clarity. However, at the time, I didn't recognize these dreams as the Lord speaking to me. In the book of Job, it addresses this;

Job 33:14-16 says, "For God may speak in one way or in another, yet man does not perceive it. In a dream, in a vision of the night, when deep sleep falls upon men, while slumbering on their beds, Then He opens the ears of men, and seal their instruction."

He spoke to me, and I did not understand it. If I had, I would have avoided much pain. I lacked knowledge of the Word, therefore I became susceptible to everything the enemy could throw at me. Because I didn't know who the Word said I was, or who God is, I became an open target.

My boyfriend told me these dreams were from the enemy, and I assumed he was right. So, I held tighter to what I wanted God to ordain. I tried to force God into a relationship He didn't want me in. Each one of my efforts failed, and the tighter I held, the more I hurt. God had already told me to put Him first, then He gave me signs as to why I should, yet I was too consumed with pleasing my boyfriend to recognize what the Lord had commanded me to do.

Despite my lack of knowledge, I still desired to know God. My passion was stirring for The Lord and it became evident in my life even after the fast had ended. As often as I could, I went to church and I began to pray even more. I began to take baby steps towards the destiny God had mapped out for me. I was searching for more of the Lord; I craved it. All I wanted was to honor Him and fall in love with Him. I tried to gain what I saw so many people had.

As I felt myself get closer to him, I unknowingly began to provoke the enemy, and attacks began to shower down upon me. As my desire grew for the Lord, fear overtook me once again. My home was no longer the peaceful relaxed environment it once was. Instead, it became a place where the enemy felt free to play.

The attacks rushed over me like a flood. My anxiety was at an all-time high as fear began to weigh heavily in my home. I began to feel uneasy sitting there in solitude, so I disrupted the lingering thoughts of darkness by surrounding myself with a new set of friends. As they'd leave, however, I was once again immersed in a sea of terror. I dreaded falling asleep, as I anticipated sleep paralysis and nightmares. Countless times, my suspenseful fears manifested into a reality. In my ignorance, I did not understand why these attacks began.

Now, I recognize how the enemy devised schemes to keep me in bondage and away from discovering my purpose and identity. The things I had become successful at hiding began to surface. Lust intensified and the feelings of homosexuality burned again in my chest. Out of all of these manifestations, the homosexual desires taunted me the most severely.

I began to sense my boyfriend was no longer interested in me the way that he claimed to be. I felt undervalued and underappreciated. I sneakily would log into his social media, only to find provocative pictures of women being sent back and forth between him and his friends. Insecurities began to choke me. I felt as if I couldn't live up to his expectations, which by his actions towards me I knew I couldn't. While that being true, he didn't just simply leave.

Yet, through these destructive emotions, neither did I.

As the days and weeks went on, I felt less and less attractive and longed-for in his eyes. The worse my perception became of myself, the wider the door was opened for the enemy to attack. I found myself wallowing in my own pity and my depleting self-esteem, when the bondage I was held in began to manifest again.

The hidden thoughts of homosexuality arose with loudness and shook the entirety of my being. The thoughts flooded my mind at full force and seemingly left me with no opportunity to escape.

Since I felt I was not receiving adequate love or affection from my boyfriend, I found it in another way. I had promised myself to never act on the thoughts, so watching porn had to once again suffice, which it did. It briefly quieted the internal chatter just enough to sustain myself in this relationship for a while longer.

Yet, a conviction tore at my soul. I felt terrible doing this, I didn't want to do this, but it felt like my only option. I couldn't fathom being released from this mental and spiritual captivity, so I became comfortable and thought I'd be bound for the rest of my life.

I did what I knew how to do and ignorantly accepted it as my truth and walked in it secretly. I plastered a smile on my face publicly in attempts to unfocus discerning and judgmental eyes. I still feared people knowing, but I had once already revealed this secret to my boyfriend.

This deeply rooted issue bothered him. His response to it was, of course, not pleasant, but after our single talk concerning it, it was never brought up again.

During this time, which was months after the conversation, I began to feel mocked. Whether it was intentional or just inconsiderate, my boyfriend reminded me of what the enemy was constantly telling me. In our relationship, "fun" was the two of us watching countless movies of his choice. These movies were typically horror-related, with this one exception.

It was a relatively good day for us, when he decided to put on a movie portraying lesbianism.

Immediately, I grew uncomfortable. Not wanting to say why, I asked to watch something else, but his persistent denials silenced my plea. I quietly felt the tears burn as they rolled down my cheek as we watched the movie. I asked once more, and with frustration, he changed it.

He questioned if it was because of the secret I once told him, but I ended the conversation by murmuring I just didn't like it. Later, once he thought I had fallen asleep, he turned the movie back on. I immediately felt like he had very little respect for me. But instead of arguing, I asked him again to watch something different. He complied, and we ended our night.

I always believed in the importance of being careful of what you watch and what you allow to enter your home. I never liked scary movies for this reason. Since childhood, I had been terrified of ghosts and demons, and certainly didn't want to entertain those fears by watching horror movies. Despite my fears, horror films were consistently being played. From the very beginning of our relationship it had been that way. Horror movies at all times, at all places. If I refused, I was manipulated into watching. He claimed it wasn't fair, and pled for me to be interested in what he watched as a child and in the things he enjoyed.

At times I fought him on it, but I usually gave in, sucking up my fears in order to be a "good" girlfriend. After watching so many of these movies, the manifestation of darkness settled into my home. He believed because it did not affect him, it shouldn't affect me either, both literally and through simply watching the movie. Yet, the more we watched, the more I was attacked.

The more weight I began to feel at home.

The more fear settled into my being.

There were times when we'd watch a scary movie, and though we agreed on him staying, he'd leave me for the evening and my anxiety would arise in my chest and sleep paralysis would torment me in the night. I remember waking up from my sleep after a disturbing dream, but was unable to move. I was pinned to the middle of my bed. my body heavily laid there as my face was forcefully shoved onto the firmness of the mattress, only my eyes were able to move. I looked to see a figure in the corner of my room staring at me. With no noise escaping my lips, I screamed the name of Jesus loudly in my spirit until I was freed.

There was no reason for it to have happened to me; my home should have been the Lord's dwelling place, His sanctuary. It was because of the things I allowed in my house that forced the spirit of God out. He only occupies where He is welcomed, and through my own and others' actions in my home, He certainly was not welcomed there.

So, there I was, left with my anxious thoughts and fears breathing down my back. I felt darkness settle into my home. I had an anxiety attack what seemed like every day. It was painful for me; the closer I got to Jesus, I felt each attack inch me back into my bondage. Still I pressed, not fully realizing the correlation.

Eventually, I got tired of my friendship circle consisting of my boyfriend and the new friends he made in the semester. Though I liked them, I needed some female companionship, someone I could vent to, someone to understand me on a new level. I was lonely, and afraid I would soon have no one at all, as he was returning to his home state after graduation.

I began to pray for the Lord to bring someone into my life, and He did. I met her in December – the same month my boyfriend was scheduled to graduate. She and I shared a similar interest in wanting to empower women. She was strong-willed and domineering, while I was still working on pushing myself out in a way that was genuine and intentional. My boyfriend's two friends who we fasted with, she, and I got along well for the most part.

When he graduated, I had people to come back to. After his graduation, I spent Christmas break with him and stayed until the spring semester began, I was turning 21 shortly after the semester was scheduled to begin so he came back to Florida with me to celebrate.

CHAPTER TWELVE

To Pray is to Win

*J*t was in 2018 when my life began to change; with every month came a drastic change. In January, on my 21st birthday, my closest friend was removed from my life because of drunken acts, lack of communication, and confusion. She was one of my constants for at least eight years, but our connection had already begun to slowly fade. After the incident on my birthday, it solidified the end of our friendship.

In the following months, God began to detach me from my boyfriend as well. My love for him was fading and I found myself relieved I didn't see him as often. I never expressed it, but being without him made me feel free. It felt like our conversations were shorter and less frequent. They lacked depth, unless he needed to talk about *his* struggles in *his* dream career.

In place of his absence, I hung out with those friends who saw me, loved me, and most importantly loved the Lord. We had Bible studies together, the four of us. It was something my spirit craved. They were what I knew to be my godly community. I looked up to these people; they inspired me and pushed me towards what God was calling me to. This was something I had not known before. I'd never had a friendship that motivated me, nor a friendship that was God-ordained, even if for a season. I started wanting more for myself, and wanting to live in purpose, seeing my friends move in surety, confidence, and joy. These are the people I began to trust with my life.

In February, my friend and I drove to my boyfriend's house to see him and watch the Superbowl with his family. Things between us were okay. We hadn't had sex since my birthday, and I intended to keep it that way. I knew he was coming down for spring break, and then again for his birthday. Since sex was always a celebratory must, I prepared myself to tell him 'no'. At this point, communication between us was very shallow. I subconsciously made myself busy, so our conversation time would be limited and because I brought a friend a long, it was easy to keep that going.

After the trip to my boyfriend's house, my school held a 3-day conference. I was reluctant about going at first, but was convinced to go by a friend.

During an altar call, with worship music filling the atmosphere, I had a vivid vision. It was God standing at the front door of my apartment. He was dressed in armor, with two swords across His chest. I also saw Him standing in the center of my room, with His back facing me, as I looked up in awe. Then, I saw Jesus in front of Him in a white robe, He and I face to face as He stares at me with peace in His eyes. To the left of us, I saw a tall and thick brick wall I could neither look over nor move.

I didn't necessarily understand this vision, but I was happy to see the Lord in this way. I was told to write it down, and I referred back to it often. It was the first of many visions I would have, but this one was perhaps the most vital one.

A month after that, God revealed it was time to experience the truth of my vision. It was time for me to move deeper with Him into a season of fighting. During those days, I prayed over my boyfriend, both for his well-being and complete salvation. I found myself fighting to discover and walk in my purpose and to pry the enemies' hands from what was rightfully mine. I was fighting to understand the calling God placed on my life and experience the ability of walking in the freedom of the Lord's light. I fought through prayer, I fought through fasting, I fought through studying the word.

I didn't fight alone though. I fought with my godly friends alongside me. With arms linked, tears in each of our eyes, we each experienced God in a new, unexplainable way. The journey lasted over a period of ten days. Each day held its own battle, but also unraveled a new piece of our individual identities as well.

Fear tried to entangle me, and I recognized my strength was not sufficient. I was forced to seek dependency upon the Lord. When chills were sent up my spine and exhaustion crept into my being, still I fought. The Lord was revealing so much to us; we couldn't grow weary. Before those days, I didn't know how to pray. It was not my strong suit, so I just didn't.

But then, more than ever, was the time to learn how. Rather than articulating my own words from my limited vocabulary and knowledge, I went to scripture. My friends and I were given a list of what I call "battle verses." I recited each one aloud with all of my might, believing there is truly power in the word of God to bring down strongholds.

As I recited these verses alongside my praying friends, the peace of God would enter my apartment and settle in the middle of my living room. Each night – each *prayer* – brought us closer to experiencing the goodness of God. Each night revealed our identity – our *God-given* identity – which we would have never known if the Lord hadn't so graciously and strategically brought us to this season. Though it was a battle we would lose using our own strength, we experienced true victory in Christ. It humbled us. It humbles me to this day, because I realized there is nothing I can accomplish without God.

He delivered the enemy into our hands to show us the power that raised Christ from the dead resides in us; we just needed to tap into it. And once we did tap into it, deliverance happened, healing happened, and restoration truly began.

It was in the midst of those ten days when I discovered the power of sharing my testimony. I was timid to walk into this battle with the secrecy of my bondage. It was one of the very first days of us praying and fasting that The Lord impressed on my heart to share what I had been dealing with the group. I felt somersaults in the pit of stomach; I was nervous, but I craved freedom more than protecting my dignity. I stood up straight, heart racing, and spoke.

"For years I have struggled with homosexuality. I've never acted on it, but it has been tormenting me for as long as I can remember." I soon discovered the thought of confessing was harder than actually confessing.

Once it was in the atmosphere, I realized what I struggled with did not diminish my value. Rather, it was a decoy the enemy used to make me think I already lacked value and would have even *less* value if I decided to speak up. I knew for years I needed to tell someone, but pride and fear always stopped me.

Confessing my struggle was more rewarding than I could ever imagine. When I released it into a safe atmosphere, it lost its power over me. It was recognized, and its spirit was now exposed with nothing to hide behind. It wanted desperately to be a part of me, and for years I perceived it *was* me, and it was simply who I was.

After I confessed, we immediately began to pray, and the Lord began to speak.

"For years," He said, "these demons have tried to attack you. They've literally been on your back, but today the Lord is freeing you. Don't ever look back."

Hearing this, I was reminded of the brick wall I saw in the vision He gave me. The Lord had already planned for this deliverance to take place, but it had to happen in the place of me seeking Him. He broke the chains of captivity, then placed mental and emotional barriers which prevented me from returning to such a place.

In the coming months, I would begin to notice how my body and mind no longer had an internal longing or reacted lustfully towards females. I was often caught by surprise when I wasn't enticed or aroused, or when the attraction was no longer present. I was almost startled by the feeling of freedom. I no longer braced myself for the racing homosexual thoughts, nor did I have a desire to throw myself back into the cycle of watching porn. I felt free from a state of mental confusion. I was in my right mind, in a *sound* mind, at least concerning the issue of homosexuality. The deliverance from it wasn't extravagant, rather I stood there, open and vulnerable with God-fearing friends, as I received healing from the Holy Spirit.

On Sunday, A few days into our spiritual fighting, my group of friends and I went to church. We were physically exhausted; we hadn't slept in days, as we stayed awake praying and fasting. We needed to be filled up again, so we went with expectancy.

On the car ride to church, I drove, as everyone else slept in the car. I had been thinking about the Lord and how I wanted more of Him. I became emotional as I let the sounds of worship play through my radio. When we got there, the worship team brought us into a time of praise and worship.

The entire time, I cried. I knew the Lord would show Himself to be faithful in the last few days of this time of fighting. I poured my heart out, seeking Him as I prayed and sang. A friend of mine came up to me and began to tell me what the Lord was telling her for me, "say yes, all He needs is your yes."

With tears stinging my eyes, I kept repeating. "Yes." I left my row and went to the altar, where I could bow in reverence and continue to pray. As I did, I looked up to see the actual glory of Jesus. It was Him, illuminated with His arms outstretched. I cried even harder in disbelief of what I was seeing. I kept saying yes and accepting Him once and for all into my heart.

That day is the day that I truly got saved.

It was immediately after those ten days when I saw my boyfriend again. I genuinely had hopes of our relationship transforming into something pleasing to God. While yes, my love for him was fading, I wanted to believe our relationship was something God could restore. Yet more than anything, I wanted to be obedient to God. I had grown too close to Him to forfeit it once more.

After the alter call, I was completely renewed. I was not the same girl he had seen just a month ago, and it showed. This new woman was not okay with her body being his playground, she was not okay with her home being the spot to get high, she was not okay with him having his way while she remained quiet. Certain things were no longer allowed in my home.

However, I lacked the authority in my voice and the confidence in my stance to simply say no. So, when my boyfriend wanted to get high, I reluctantly told him he could.

Right then, I felt the Lord convict me. How could I tell God to dwell in my home while allowing what was not pleasing to Him to reside also?

I laid on my bed, powerless, as he got high on the patio. Instead of fully taking the Lord's conviction upon myself, I justified my lack of action by placing the blame on him. I laid there and thought, "that's none of my business. That's between him and God." But, those thoughts weren't true, because I was responsible for allowing it in my home.

A friend of mine, who was also with me in the midst of those ten days praying and fasting, sat on the couch confused as to why I was allowing this to happen. She texted me to quietly and discreetly confront me, but also to encourage me. After our conversation, I went to the bathroom and began to pray, because I truthfully was not happy. I was over both his *and* my behavior.

I asked him to come in my room and told him smoking in my home could no longer happen and I didn't want weed in my house either. Of course, defenses shot up, and he immediately tried to silence my request.

I relinquished everything I could do or say and became an empty vessel for the Lord to speak through. After what seemed to be an hours-long outburst full of accusations, tears, and ridiculous requests on his part, he complied as I pried the bud out of his tear-drenched hand and flushed it down the toilet.

This moment, for me, was important because it was the first time I truly stood up for myself and something I believed in. I didn't let his words or tears manipulate me into shrinking due to his request. But of course, this brought an unexplainable amount of tension to our relationship.

That night, we slept separately. I let him have the bed as I slept on the couch with my friend. I couldn't be near him. I was proud of myself, but also needed to clear my mind.

The next morning, I went into the room to see him staring back at me. He asked why I didn't sleep with him and I shrugged, uninterested in explaining myself or actions. Still, he took it as an opportunity to further the conversation. I yielded to it, curious of what his heart and mind held.

He felt as though I was trying to push him to be at a place spiritually he simply was not ready to be at. He was right. I was out of love, because a part of me still wanted him, but in a way which would fit with my relationship with God. I realized I could not change him to be the man I wanted him to be. I also recognized that he wasn't the man for me. I realized I shouldn't have to *want* to change the man who was built for me. It wasn't fair to me, or to him, and I simply deserved better.

As we spoke, he admitted to dealing with some hidden pain and the fact I wanted to change him hurt him more. Knowing my only option, I took it as my opportunity to end the relationship on the premise of him seeking the healing he needed and deserved. I simply wanted the best of him, no longer the potential of him. I figured if we were meant to be, the Lord would truly bring us back together after we discovered and began to walk as the version of ourselves the Lord desired for us to be.

While peace embraced me, anguish crushed him. As I looked at the misery on his face, tears rolled down my cheeks. I wanted to swallow the words I just let into the atmosphere, but couldn't. I stood my ground, knowing it was for the best. Immediately, he pleaded for me to take back what I had suggested.

Taken aback by his refusal, I listened to what else he had to say. I had very little argument, other than, "you need healing, and I don't want to hurt you more than you are hurt." He counteracted it by exclaiming how desperately he *needed* me.

Yet, the gut feeling remained. In that moment I understood that I still wasn't *wanted*, but rather I was his possession who could do things for him and even perhaps encourage him when he *needed* me. He told me I didn't need to carry his burdens all these years, even though they were carelessly thrown upon me. He made it my fault for feeling weighed down and overwhelmed by him during the duration of our relationship.

The conversation itself exhausted me. I half-listened as he explained to me how he wasn't ready to walk in the light of salvation until he could decide that he was ready himself not because *I* wanted him to be ready. He claimed he was so close to that point, but I essentially ruined it by forcing God on him. Especially in the area of him not smoking. He was adamant about coming to the end of this dependency for weed on his terms, but my spirit knew it was false.

I refused to feel guilty for not allowing certain things in my home. I kindly disagreed with him and told him how God was not a God of confusion, and if the end of his dependency was supposed to happen, there'd be peace surrounding the decision, but there wasn't.

Throughout the conversation, I felt uneasy, but it wasn't until he made one of his final statements when the state of my spirit was eradicated. We were both sitting in the middle of my bedroom floor when he looked me in the eyes and said he only fears two things in the world.

"What?" I asked.

"God and losing you."

Something about his statement startled my spirit. It felt unnatural, almost possessive. In all, it felt untrue; nothing about his character or actions showed he had a fear of the Lord. Yet throughout the conversation, he kept claiming he was truly a man of God.

Following his statement, I inched backwards and I tilted my head in doubt and confusion.

"Don't be afraid, I know, that's a lot of love."

I'm not sure what startled me the most about the statement: the dishonesty in it, or the fact he believed it to be true. But what disturbed my spirit so intensely was how I was in the same category as God.

I put the conversation aside for the sake of peace. One night, however, as he was sitting on my patio, alone in a dining room chair. I felt obligated to text him to make sure he was fine. He denied explaining that he was overwhelmed, saying "I can't believe you tried to do that yesterday."

I felt guilty. He was clearly hurting, he *needed* me. So, I apologized. He continued to hope our relationship would be transformed, apart of me did too. His stay came to an end and I drove him to the airport. On our way there I told him how important it was to become dependent on the Lord. I didn't want to continue to be in a Godless relationship and I didn't want him to continue in his bondage. He listened. He even finally agreed.

CHAPTER THIRTEEN

HE Released Me

*O*ver the next few days, we talked regularly over text and FaceTime. Yet, I could sense his dedication to the words he told me at the airport weren't as genuine as I initially perceived.

He disliked that I was on a "spiritual high", as he defined my encounter with God to be. He used my growth as a measuring stick to discredit and devalue himself. I refused to be manipulated or feel guilty. I refused to shrink. I remained in the joy of the Lord and continued to speak. Even in the one-sided conversation, still I hoped. I hoped things would change. I hoped he would find himself and find the Lord the more we talked about what the Lord had done for me. Still, despite my efforts and my allowing the Lord to use me, the tension between us was strong enough to crack our phone screens. It was evident, and so very tangible, despite his occasional "uh-huh" and "okay".

After I got off of the phone, a friend who was at my house during that time asked me what I was holding onto in the relationship at this point. I dug deep, realizing love had not been a factor, rather our relationship hung onto the frail strings of a hope of reached potential, and of a fresh start. But, the hope weighed on every part of me. It stagnated me, and as I uttered those words to my friend, I knew it was time to cut off what I held onto for so long.

That same night, she and I discussed how the relationship was coming to an end in the near future, and I came to terms with it. I began distancing myself as he texted me trying to get my attention and sympathy; I replied with dryness, and without my usual tendency to overextend myself to ease the bondage of his mind.

He texted me asking if I could pray, telling me it was difficult for him to breathe due to a bronchitis flareup. It was 4am. Typically, I would've ran to his side in prayer, but this time, I glanced at the text and placed my phone back down. There was no urgency in my heart; rather, it was quite the opposite. I knew he was, or at least would be okay. I refused to retreat to the space I was delivered from. I would no longer be his landing grounds of his emotional baggage. I would not feel bad nor be manipulated to change how I felt about this particular thing. So with that, my friend and I ended our conversation and I went to bed.

The next day, I made up my mind: the relationship was truly over. However, I decided to wait on the Holy Spirit to show me how and when to end it.

After my classes, I had more peace about my coming decision and I shared it with the other two who prayed and fought with me spiritually just two weeks prior.

The first one I saw always brought me joy and peace when I was around him, and my heart was in need of refreshing. As I approached him, he greeted me with a hug and I told him.

"I'm breaking up with him."

He had known the things I had gone through, more in-depth than even I did. So, after sharing my heart on the matter, he immediately supported my decision.

In regards to my boyfriend, however, I still hadn't ended it. I was waiting on instructions from the Lord, so as he texted me question marks in regard to not answering the previous night, I played it off by redirecting the conversation.

I eventually got too deep into my own conversations at school to even remember to text him back. I suppose he noticed the inconsistencies in my texting, and questioned whether I'd be busy or not that day. He asked me this because I hadn't been giving him the attention he desired. Yet, why lie?

"Yeah, I will be," I responded after telling him my plans for the day. I sent him the message at 2:42 pm My anticipation was increasing to end the relationship, but I knew I shouldn't rush, because the Lord's timing would be perfect. I placed my phone back down and continued speaking and receiving revelation from the Lord in our conversation about my relationship.

Eventually, my other friend came to encourage and speak life into me, and also to warn me about the backlash of my decision. Soon our other friend who encouraged me the night before also joined us.

Within the next hour, my boyfriend began to text me about events from the past week which had deeply bothered and affect him. I felt bad, but no words would form for me to respond to him. I let my phone buzz with alerts constantly, until the Lord finally dropped words on my heart to say to him. Words that I knew didn't come from my me.

At last, at 4:34 P.M, after wrestling with the Lord, I typed, "I can't be with you anymore."

My heart raced and my stomach turned, but I quickly hit send. Immediately as I did, peace rushed over me. I turned on 'Do Not Disturb,' because I knew he'd try to reach me, but I had nothing more to say.

That night, I celebrated freedom in the presence of the Lord. My friends and I attended a worship night at our church. As the music beat through the speakers and heavenly melodies filled the air, I couldn't help but to dance and grin in the presence of the Lord. I believe the song which was playing, was really for me. I needed it.

The song spoke about the joy of the Lord being my everlasting and constant strength that no one could steal from me. The joy of the Lord was not like my innocence which was robbed or the thoughts in my mind which often felt distorted. The joy of the Lord is a gift not based upon circumstances but freely given to those who accept Him and that night, I jumped, twirled and danced in His joy.

I sang that song with passion as the truth stirred up within my spirit. We entered into a slower time of worship, and I remember simply bowing my head in prayer. As I prayed, I felt an inclination from the Lord on my heart. He dropped a few words on my heart, and though I did not hear them verbally, I felt them in the pit of my spirit, the same place I had heard "I can't be with you" just earlier in the day. The words were simple, but they weren't for me; they were for my friend standing next to me.

I wrestled back and forth within myself, still unfamiliar with the voice of the Lord. The words felt like a weight repeatedly being pushed down on my chest. Still, I said nothing. Fear and intimidation of being wrong silenced me. As I saw her begin to move towards who God had asked her to go to, I was crushed by a wave of regret. I doubted God's voice, though it seemed so clear. The room still dim and worship filling the air. I asked the Lord to forgive me for being disobedient and not recognizing His voice. My heart was truly saddened I missed an opportunity of obedience out of doubt and fear. Still, I sought him through my discouragement.

I stood there in the presence of the Lord, occasionally bowing in reverence or lifting my hands in praise. I was finally free. Despite my disobedience for staying in that relationship as long as I did, I still felt the Lord's grace over me. He was still proud of me, and still had a word for me. My ears snapped out of my inner thoughts and silent prayers as the Pastor walked onto the stage with a few words to say. I slipped my phone out of my back pocket to take some notes. Knowing whatever he had to say would be directly from the heart of the Lord.

I waited in anticipation until I heard the word I had come for. The Lord was saying, not only to me, but to the whole congregation: "Yes, I will take you deeper. You are entering into a new season where you will go deeper."

I smiled as I quickly typed those words down. Just earlier in the day, I had prayed, asking the Lord to take me deeper. I didn't understand the fullness of what it meant; I just knew I wanted more of what God had to offer. I continued to worship and pray well past midnight, until we were released from the event.

As we were leaving, we were prompted to turn around, to finish receiving all the Lord wanted to implant within us. As we reentered the sanctuary, I made my way back up to the front, which was once filled with desperate hearts, but now only held a few lingering worshipers.

I stood there, in awe of the beauty of how the Lord moved. The room felt pure and peaceful. I was reminded of how the waves caress the shore gently, then retreat, pulling any inhabitants of the sand back into the water. I realized it was what the Lord does; he gently pulls you in, then submerges you in his love, bringing you deeper and deeper with every current.

My heart smiled as I waited in his presence with joy, writing down poems, praises, and notes from the service. Afterwards, I glanced up from my phone and began to look around the room once more. My eyes landed on the screens, which read "Presence night – creating space for God to move."

The statement stirred something deep down inside of me. I began to write again.

"Move things around," I wrote. "There is too much cluster in the way for God, and God will only enter a place of comfort and holiness. Clean out so that He can move."

This statement related to so many areas of my life, but at the time, I had not truly realized it. To me, it was nothing more than just a statement I wrote. However, looking back now, I believe it was instructions from the Lord. Although I was freshly out of my relationship, there were tangible, mental, emotional, and spiritual things I needed to be detoxed from. I was not developing into my full identity because I had been connected to the wrong source for so long.

The pastor, simply yet profoundly, spoke on this issue. He said at times, we are in a dry place because of our connection to another dry place. My dry place, of course, was the relationship with my now ex-boyfriend. I wasn't seeing the promises of God in my life because of what I attached myself to.

With this revelation, I needed to know my next moves, in regards to my now ex-boyfriend. I already had no peace in speaking to him, so I refused to respond to his multiple text messages or phone calls. Then, the Lord being so gracious and faithful, brought a friend to me to give me a verse the Lord had placed on her heart: Ecclesiastes 3:1-8.

"To everything there is a season, a time for every purpose under heaven. A time to be born and a time to die; A time to plant and a time to pluck what is planted; A time to kill and a time to heal; A time to break down and a time to build up; A time to weep and a time to laugh; A time to mourn and a time to dance; A time to cast away stones and a time to gather stones; A time to embrace and a time to refrain from embracing; A time to gain and a time to lose; A time to keep and a time to throw away; A time to tear and a time to sew; A time to keep silence and a time to speak; A time to love and a time to hate; A time of war, And a time of peace (NKJV)."

As I read this passage, a confirmation to remain silent settled into my spirit. After April 3, 2018, I never spoke to him again. Thus beginning my journey of going deeper with the Lord.

CHAPTER FOURTEEN

Newness From the Depth

*D*uring the next few days, I recognized the acuteness of my silence. I had received countless calls, texts, DM's, and eventually an email from my ex, none of which I responded to. After his many failed attempts, his friends and family tried to contact me as well. Some confessed their true thoughts and feelings about me and the relationship, others softly inquired about the cause of the breakup. The rest angrily demanded to know what happened.

I was overwhelmed at this point, and I didn't feel at liberty to speak to any of them. I suppose when they noticed I would not be returning any calls or messages, they took it upon themselves to contact my friends and family. I let all of the messages and calls I received pile up. I refused to reply to anyone without knowing how long my season of silence would last.

I was sitting in my psychology class, needing clarity from the Lord, when the verse-of-the-day notification popped up, catching my attention. I opened the Bible app and began to read Joshua 23:9-13. By ending up on this exact scripture, I knew it was by the grace and provision of God. Before this, I had never read something which struck me as intensely as this.

As I read, I felt my world shift. I had not only been given my answer, but a warning as well. The verse read,

"So be very careful to love the Lord your God. But if you turn away from Him and cling to the customs of the survivors of these nations remaining among you, and if you intermarry with them, then know for certain that the Lord your God will no longer drive them out of your land. Instead, they will be a snare and a trap to you, a whip for your backs and thorny brambles in your eyes, and you will vanish from this good land the Lord your God has given you."

Essentially, the Lord was telling me to continue to diligently seek and abide in Him and refrain from going back to what he had just taken me out of. It was through His strength that I was able to exit the relationship. By His power, strength, and my obedience I would stay out. In this, He began to warn me: if I were to go back or even consider being friends with him, it would lead to my own destruction.

He left me voicemails, promising change. Though a piece of my heart wanted to give in to his plea, the Holy Spirit stopped me. Something seemingly so innocent would have turned back into a cycle, where I'd once again be trapped in the palm of manipulation. As this revelation settled in the depth of my spirit, the Lord began to reveal even more.

What is done, said, and thought in the dark will always come to light rang in my head. I wasn't sure why, but I had jotted it down in my notes anyway.

Throughout the week, things began to bubble up to the surface. The smoke-filled secrets which were shared on my apartment patio began to be revealed. The dream I had concerning the girl kissing him was a warning sign from the Lord, showing me the reality of my suspicions. For those two and a half years, I didn't see myself as special to him, as attractive, as valued, or respected. All at once, the Lord showed me I surely was none of those things in his eyes. I was even shown how I truly got an STD just a year prior.

Upon the revelation of these things, I wasn't hit with pain immediately. Though I was cautioned the pain of the reality would eventually come, it still hadn't pierced my already-fragile heart. Truthfully, I blocked out thoughts of him altogether - I subconsciously numbed myself. I focused my attention on my friends, who distracted me from feeling the heartbreak. Two of my friends from the days of fasting and praying stayed with me for the remaining month of our spring semester.

During this month, I purged my house of everything that reminded me of my ex. I gathered bags of his belongings and got rid of every last one of his remaining things. The process was liberating; it was emotionally freeing. Selling his things was admittedly at the forefront of my mind, but the Lord had shown me how difficult it would be for me to see others in my area wearing his things. So, I threw them away to prevent me from ever seeing them again.

In it, I didn't only throw his things but some of mine as well. Things that he'd *seen* me in, things I owned and he liked, things he even bought me.

Was it petty? Maybe. But it was for my own sanity. I couldn't give the enemy any room to play with my mind by reminding me of what once was when I slipped on a shirt that was from him or sipped tea from a mug he gave me. Anything that reeked of the residue of our relationship, I avoided, and eliminated all opportunities for bitter reminders.

Immediately after the breakup, I took practical steps to ensure we truly remained broken-up. Prior to this, I had read a trending story on social media of a young woman who walked into her boyfriend's home and caught him asleep and naked with another woman. Rather than letting loose in a destructive outburst, she exited the home and the relationship with class.

As she left, the story read, she sat in her car and called her phone company to have her number changed, blocked him on all social media accounts, changed the locks to her apartment, and informed her friends and family about the decision she'd made.

For some reason, when I read it, it stuck with me; it empowered me. I was in awe of this woman's strength in a generation where fights break loose over gaining the attention of an undeserving man. She broke the norm by not adding more fuel to the fire with her anger, and she simply exited the burning building of her broken relationship.

In this month, her story kept replaying in my mind. I caught myself following in her brave and unusual footsteps.

I called my cell phone company and changed my number. I informed my friends and family as to why I did it, and they supported me.

I blocked him from all of my social media accounts.

Then, I remembered I had loaned him a key to my apartment. While he was in another state, he still essentially had access to me. I took the extra step and changed my locks.

Why did I go so extreme? Should I have not? With no ring on my finger and no child in my womb, I recognized my obligation was to no one. It was in obedience to what the Lord had told me to do.

Most days, I stayed strong. I avoided unblocking him and looking at his social media account, and I spent more time with the friends I had developed in the prior season. Even with him being in another state and all of the precautions I had taken, I did not want to be alone. I was afraid my ex would pop up. I also felt like the minute I were alone, I would get spiritually attacked.

So, I attempted to protect myself from those things by essentially hiding behind my two friends until the end of the semester. They were both with me leading up to the breakup, and I felt safe with them. I could be open, honest, and just have *fun*.

Summer came, and I spent the first few weeks with one of those friends. Consumed by our time together, I neglected the season the Lord desired to bring me into. After all that I had been through, I needed to be cleansed, redefined and renewed by the Lord. Up until this point I had no idea who Ashley even was.

I was the girl that people knew because they knew the people I hung out around. I was no more than a shadow, a whisper rather than a voice and a person who needed the validation of others to survive. I didn't know me. I suffocated the newness trying to arise out of me with adventure fun and crushes. Even after the hell I went through in my past relationship. I wasn't equipped to be around others but still here I was - blinded to that truth doing what I did best, smiling as I numbly walk through my life.

After a few weeks of drowning in distractions, the Lord began to give me revelation about the next chapter in my life. The season I was entering would be the most important season of my life and I could not risk being distracted, because in this season I would learn to have a relationship with the Lord. From there, the Lord would take me places I couldn't imagine for myself. I needed to trust Him and yield everything I was to Him. I was told to go home and relieve myself of distractions to seek Him. That particular night the Lord quenched my dried spirit with affirmations, promises, and instructions.

While I felt so much happiness with those friends, they distracted me from both my relationship with the Lord and the direction in which I was meant to walk. It became clear as to why the Lord sent me home and us our different ways.

In the following days, I developed an intense hunger for the Lord, one unlike anything I had ever experienced before. I constantly wanted revelation and a word from the Lord, so I sought after those things. I dedicated myself to reading the word. I laid in bed all day, just listening to the word and reading along from the Bible app on my phone.

I felt a new me emerging. My spirit was beginning to wake up inside me, and I was refreshed by its dedication to the Lord. During this time, prayer became my first language. I prayed constantly; I couldn't help but to. It was as though something inside of me would tighten up, and I would not receive a release until an 'amen' rolled off my lips. My prayers became uncontrollable, my tongue feeling like it was on fire, but it's what put my spirit man back at ease. I remember praying this way a few times before in worship settings – but this time, I knew it came directly from the heart of the Father, as I prayed things only He would know about.

One of the first times I felt the urgency to pray was one evening when the sky was settling into a purple hue and the air was still humid from the recent downpour. I saw a full rainbow, and something in me wanted to chase the sunset.

I was in my car driving at this point, and as I drove, I felt the need to go home, so I took my exit, putting me in the opposite direction of the sunset. My heart raced with awe and sadness; the glorious sight had disappeared, but to my surprise, as I pulled into my complex, the sunset was hovering over my building, in the most beautiful shade I had ever seen.

I ran upstairs, awestruck by the Lord's creation, put on some worship music, and prayed. I prayed until I ran out of things to say. I'd never prayed as long as

I had; two minutes was possibly my maximum time, but this time, it felt like more. I kept going, then prayed even more later. I stopped when I realized how long I'd prayed, and felt like it was enough.

Still, my spirit still hungered to meet the Lord in the place of prayer. I fell asleep, but woke up with a heart softened to the Lord and still wanting more. I continued to practice having a prayer life and reading the word, I was beginning to actually enjoy it, it was becoming a part of me not simply as a routine but as a lifestyle.

At this time, I was anticipating going to a conference in a few weeks. I was very eager for it, and one of my close friends at the time was coming down to attend as well.

The week before the conference, I lost my voice. I got laryngitis for the first time in my life, and couldn't speak at all. I was not only terrified because of the discomfort of not being able to speak, but I was also disheartened because I wanted to be able to pray and worship at this conference.

Saddened I ignored the Lords call to rest in His presence that day. Later that evening, I did pray finding my way back to Him even though I initially wanted to wallow in self-pity. The next few days I continued to pray, but in my thoughts. Although I knew I could pray in my in this way, it just didn't seem as powerful to me, but evidently, the Lord hears even the quietest of prayers. I prayed in my thoughts moving my lips as though words were coming out. I prayed for healing, so I may be able to pray and worship for the upcoming three days, when I would be at conference.

A couple of days before the conference began, and my voice was starting to come back. Those days passed slowly and conference finally arrived. As I drove to the church, anticipation was pounding in my chest. I *expected* something, I wanted to receive a word which would change me. By the faithfulness of God, I did.

At every. Single. Session

CHAPTER FIFTEEN

Remnant

*C*onference was the most amazing event I had ever experienced. Every doubt, question, and thought pertaining my relationship with God was answered in the most unexpectedly beautiful ways. I was there the first night, the room blackened with only speckles from bright lights from the stage. The atmosphere was still, but my ears rang from the wails of desperation. Some pleaded to experience the presence of the Lord, while others sobbed from the weight of His glory resting upon them.

I, kneeling in a cramped space on the floor, began to worship as well. In that moment, I recognized I was a novice when it came to worship. What were the techniques, the correct posture, the right words to say when the singers had brief moments of silence? I felt as though I was doing it wrong, and it bothered me.

Was there a correct way to worship? I didn't know, but in that moment I was pressuring myself to cry from a place of evidence. I wanted to prove to the Lord I *felt* something, but my eyes remained dry. I was so focused on my lack of emotion, I didn't have the opportunity to truly surrender myself to worship the Lord. I rocked back and forth on my knees, quietly praying and calling on the name of Jesus. *Nothing.*

I sighed in defeat, as if I did something wrong. I felt inadequate. I wanted to be desperate for his presence, but I felt as though I had fallen short because I wasn't *feeling* the preciousness you're *supposed* to feel. The feeling you get when you *know* the Holy Spirit has entered the room.

Although the weight of His glory had yet to fall over me, I still believed He was there. The reaction of other worshippers proved it, but I wanted to experience Him myself.

As worship continued, I kept pushing myself, occasionally slipping away in futile thought, but always ushered myself back to a place of worship and prayer. As worship came to a close, I slowly returned to my seat, bothered I hadn't felt His presence and feeling as though I had worshipped in vain.

During this moment of condemnation, it was as though the Lord swooped in and revealed to me the truth of worship. One of the pastors in the service humbly came to stage with a word of encouragement. For me, it was a word from the Lord.

He clarified worship was *not* a matter of feeling. I had it all wrong, I had mistakenly made worship about what I felt, when worship is truly the only thing I as a believer can offer the Lord. I was humbled, and excited to understand I had not done anything wrong. Worship was a way to express my gratitude, love, and reverence to God, and I had finally been freed from the lie telling me I simply was not a worshipper. The truth is, I am a worshipper, and *this fact* made my spirit come alive.

The following nights, and every worship experience I've had since then, were different. I had to continue to push myself, but as I did, the Lord graciously gave me more and more revelations and understanding of worship. I was becoming a woman of prayer, and as I grew into this identity, I understood worship to be a form of guided prayer - according to a missionary I once heard. Since then, I began to make every song become a personal truth for me, and I've experienced transformation in my worship life.

It began, *truly began*, at conference.

As the night progressed, the Lord kept speaking to me. I had an intense knowing in the pit of my stomach: the word being preached was designed for my ears to hear, and soul to grab ahold of. The pastor preached on us, babies in the faith, finally taking serious steps towards living fully for the Lord. I felt targeted by the Holy Spirit. The revelation sank into my heart and I pondered on my life. For as long as I could remember, specifically throughout my college years, the Lord had been calling out to me and trying to get and *keep* my attention. While my heart desired the Lord, I still dismissed the yearning to actually put in the work to develop a relationship with Him.

The passage being preached was Luke 13:6-9. It read:

"Then Jesus told this story: 'A man planted a fig tree in his garden and came again and again to see if there was any fruit on it but he was always disappointed. Finally, He said to his gardener, "I've waited *three years*, and there hasn't been a single fig! Cut it down. It's just taking up space in the garden' The gardener answered, 'Sir, give it one more chance. Leave it another year, and I'll give it special attention and plenty of fertilizer. If we get figs next year then fine, if not then you can cut it down.'"

For me, it truly had been three years. Three years since I decided I wanted a new beginning. Three years since I was baptized. Three years since I decided I didn't want to live in sin anymore. But those three years were ineffective. For three years little had changed for me spiritually, and all of my *deciding* to live for the Lord was in vain as they were not supported with any action.

As I sat, listening to the message, an urgency developed within me, signifying it was time. The mercy of Christ had protected me countless of times, but now I was in between the third and fourth year of the Lord calling me by name, and the Holy Spirit was telling me now was the time to either produce, or be cut down. It was time to not only say yes to Him, but also a time to produce the fruit He was expecting from me, time to make a *real* decision.

I humbly realized I am not the Lord's only option. If I continued to deny His call over my life, I would simply be given over to the hardness of my heart. I would ultimately be cut down, stripped of what I was *supposed* to be because of fear and insecurities.

So, here it was, my final invitation, the Lord's hand still lovingly stretched out for me to grasp and make the choice to follow Him. Afraid, uncertain, and convicted, I said "yes" to follow Him, and "yes" to produce the fruit He patiently waited for from me.

With fire in my veins and determination in my heart, I went to the next few services, worshipping and seeking Him differently than I had before. My heart was ready to receive as I sat in the seat waiting to hear the word the Lord had for me.

The message was all about the waiting process before spiritual elevation. I wasn't sure where God was calling me, but in the meantime, I knew I couldn't be lazy, and I needed to be a good steward over the little things I had been trusted with in my life. Even while in the mix of being faithful and obedient, I, like Elisha, did not need to stress over what my mantle was or when it would come. I was learning that through my faithfulness, the mantle - whatever it was- would find me.

The pastor powerfully articulated how in order to walk in more authority and power, then my lifestyle must be situated in a way those things could be sustained. I *did* want more, but I was a bit afraid as to what it would entail. If I'm honest, I tended to be lazy.

As he preached, he explained the process of being faithful enough to qualify for elevation. First, was to be content with the mantle I would be given and to also destroy whatever alternative plan.

This statement alone touched me. I had never *truly and completely* known what I would be. I had guesses and things I thoughtlessly had chosen. The statement, however, gave me confidence. I had nothing to fall back on, so it essentially forced me to follow the direction of Lord over my life.

The pastor then went on to explain the mission of believers, which was to contend in prayer and fasting for the things the Lord had spoken over their life because there is an enemy who would love to keep me from building and advancing in the things of the Lord.

Lastly, and perhaps most difficult, I had to surrender and give up control of the process, and to stay in pace with the twists and turns of my life, which would come from following the Lord.

That service ended and I quickly left to get lunch as a friend and I unpacked what was just spoken. There was still more, I sensed it in my spirit.

Within the next hour, I found myself back in the sanctuary, excited for the next message to come. This one discussed the importance of having reverence and a sense of awareness for the presence of the Lord. He tackled the issue of distraction and passivity in a moment of worship – two of the things I had dealt with in frequently in worship settings.

The Lord does not enter a room for no reason; He is there to speak, act, or both. It is up to me as an individual to decide whether I will have an encounter with Him. It depends on my posture and my unwavering hunger.

The service ended with an intense and beautiful prayer. We prayed in groups, and then individually for a while. It was the most fulfilling thing I had experienced. The anointing in the room was as thick as the oil produced from the pressing of olives.

I was taught to take advantage of every moment when the Lord enters a room, and to push and not miss my visitation. Even if the visit is simply to be immersed in His presence, even if I heard no words and nothing visibly miraculous happened, I should not miss His presence. So, I pressed as I prayed, throat still strained from being sick, pushing past the discomfort.

As the service extended into the night, the final pastor of the conference came to the stage. He was someone who I had been watching for a few months at the time, Pastor Mike Todd. I was ecstatic, and prayed for a good word, one that spoke directly to me. From the beginning, my attention was captivated. My heart stood at attention ready to receive the wisdom and instructions I *knew* the Lord had for me.

I had been to several conferences before in my life, and each time, I would feel fire beneath my feet as I planned to continue my race towards Jesus. Yet, before a prayer could even form on my tongue I was consumed by the troubles of my world and slipped back into the identity of complacency and naive routine. This time around I was afraid the same would happen. It had been an issue on my heart for the past few weeks and the question floating in my mind was how - how do I sustain this fire.

God, being God, knew my fear. He took my feelings into deep consideration, He instructed Pastor Mike to enlighten me on how to continue to strive towards Him after the conference came to an end. The service began with him first describing the current generational epidemic of what he called *faith fatigue*. With the question of how still in my mind, the Lord began to speak to me and tell me what to do. Through Pastor Mike He explained that faith fatigue happens upon leaving a powerful moment and returning home, only to be disappointed because your prayers hadn't manifested in the immediate way you expect. This causes faith to become sick - attacking our spiritual stamina. The very thing I had faced so many times finally was being given a name and an answer.

Proverbs 13:12, in The Passion Translation, says "When hope's dream seems to drag on and on, the delay can be depressing. But when at last your dreams come true, life's sweetness will satisfy your soul." I understand what it means to feel frustration and sadness creep on you as you wait for the thing you've been praying for. It becomes disheartening, as if God isn't listening and then we stop. Stop praying, stop seeking, stop waiting. But as the Pastor explained, there are vital steps to keep the faith in the midst of the waiting. I was intrigued, vigorously typing notes down in my phone. I needed to know how to fight like the woman in Luke who kept asking the judge over and over for something until he gave in. I wanted to be like *her*. I wanted to beat faith fatigue.

First and foremost, the pastor stressed the issue of having a godly community surrounding you. This community is a set of people who will hold you up when the enemy has tried to knock you off of your feet. They will be there, arms linked and chests out, ready to help you withstand the tricks and attacks that come while chasing after the Lord. Without these people, you are more likely to fall into the trap of isolation, fear, depression, or whatever else the enemy can use to mislead you about your identity. As it is written in Ecclesiastes 4:9-12 (NIV),

"Two are better than one, because they have a good return for their labor: If either of them falls down, one can help the other up. But pity anyone who falls and has no one to help them up. Also, if two lie down together, they will keep warm. But how can one keep warm alone? Though one may be overpowered, two can defend themselves. A cord of three strands is not quickly broken."

I smiled, I shouted, I jumped up and down, remembering how I stood, arms locked, hunched over, interceding with my friends, who Lord had given me, as I prayed my way out of the toxic relationship I was in. *I had it, I finally had it*, I thought to myself.

As he continued to be used by the Lord, the pastor finally released the steps I had anticipated. I took out my phone and took notes – Talk to God on a daily basis; Have agreement with others about the things you are praying for; Extend your prayers among yourself - pray for others; Grow in devotion and quiet time with the Lord; Ask God again for what you initially asked; Pray until it turns into a praise.

These points all cleverly spelled out THE GAP. This was my daily game plan; it would be the foundation of me developing a devotional and deeper prayer life. It was *so* simple, but it was exactly what I needed to hear.

It was the most *beautiful* night I had ever experienced. I was grateful, I was excited, and I was ready to put action behind my "yes". As the Holy Spirit continued to minister to people throughout the sanctuary, an old friend of mine from high school came up to me. We hadn't spoken in years, and I was surprised he even remembered me. He came up to me and handed me a note that read:

"God keeps reminding you this weekend of parts of your story, so never forget what God's love was willing to do to pursue you and never leave you! The next season God is calling you to, is dependent on remembering your only qualification is God's love for you. This must not be shaken. You have not missed it or squandered it away! This weekend was designed for you."

My heart beamed. It was such an encouragement and so sweet of the Lord to speak to me in this way. So gentle, *so precious*. This note made my night; despite my shame, filth, and bondage I once wallowed in, I was reminded that I hadn't been disqualified from God's love. I hurried home and hung this note up in my room, so I could constantly be reminded of its truth.

The next morning, I made my way to the final worship experience of the conference. I stood in the far back and worshipped until multiple pastors made their way to the stage. I excitedly sat down to listen to what they had to say.

Unlike the other sessions, there wasn't a sermon; rather, a question-and-answer service was being held. I sat happily, my spirit quietly declaring *Glory to God for the upcoming revelations.* Questions from the audience began to flood in and wisdom was eloquently dispelled from the stage. I noted everything which was spoken, but my heart stopped as a question I'd grappled with for a while was read.

"How do I know it's God, and not my own thoughts?"

The first answer we were given was to develop a private and personal relationship with the Lord, which typically consisted of journaling, a quiet space, and of course, consistency. That, I could do. Yet, how could I hear his voice? I was surrounded by people who heard the voice of the Lord frequently and easily. I often would feel incredibly discouraged because I hadn't heard Him in the same way.

The pastor began to explain it, how a father would speak to each child differently, so the Lord speaks to each of us. God is proven to speak in visions, thoughts, dreams, or an impression on the heart. All my life, I supposed that I would hear His voice like loud thunder rolling in the sky. I anticipated that way alone and dismissed all other forms that the Lord had spoken to me, thus, creating the frustrating belief that I was spiritually deaf.

But the truth was, I was spiritually unaware I had never been taught how to hear Him or to distinguish His voice from my thoughts. These answers began to feel like the missing piece I needed in my relationship with the Lord.

Another pastor began to speak and my attention gravitated towards him. He explained how the Lord speaks firstly according to His Word. Meaning, if what we heard does not line up with the Bible, then it certainly was *not* God. God is not the author of confusion (1 Corinthians 14:33) nor is He Himself confused. He would *never* tell you to do something contradictory to what His word says.

As the pastor continued, he explained God will also speak with persistence; it will be a recurring impression or thought, constantly tugging at you even after you put it to the side.

He speaks in the midst of a random moment, typically when we weren't dwelling on something. It drops in our mind or spirit. All of these were examples of the voice of the Lord, all of which I had heard or received. Yet, my problem was, I hadn't *recognized* the simplicity of His voice. The session eventually ended and I locked my phone, pondering on all of the revelations I had been given.

The entire conference was wrapped by in a moment of prayer. As individual murmurs of prayers filled the room, I had a vision.

I saw myself in my apartment, kneeling on the floor, praying as I clutched onto a book. The one I held onto was one out of many, the rest filling a brown box that sat near me. I saw passion and intensity as I watched myself pray fervently over this book. As I watched, I realized that the book was one that I had written.

The time had come. The Lord was pushing me to write a book, just months before this moment I declared that I would be a published author. At the time of the statement, I hadn't discovered my deeply hidden love for the Lord, so I hadn't known this idea was from Him. But now, at the sight of my vision, I knew it was Him all along. Now, *specifically now*, was go time.

CHAPTER SIXTEEN

A Way In The Wilderness

I left the conference, excited to begin my walk with the Lord and to write the book He'd placed in my heart. Conference had truly transformed me and directed my steps in the way in which I needed to go. Conference gave me clarity, vision and purpose. I had already begun writing earlier in the year, but distractions hindered my discipline from ever getting anything done. Now, there was an urgency in me to write this book.

I had begun to be questioned if I had been writing, I listened to sermons which prompted listeners to write what the Lord had instructed them to, and multiple other people were inquiring when I'd be publishing a book. I was shocked by the confirmations, and eager to begin.

Yet, every time it crossed my mind to do it, I would be half-hearted about it. I wasn't in the atmosphere that I needed to be in to truly work on my purpose. The atmosphere and my mindset was so off that I struggled to even seek the Lord at my fullest potential. I knew the Lord would require separation and consecration from me. Still, I found myself back in the face of others rather than God.

One afternoon I was prompted to write something that had been on my heart that I had not verbalized. It was a short simple statement - "I want to be alone. I *need* to be alone." Conviction rested heavily on my chest day and night. For the entire summer, I had hardly done a single thing the Lord needed me to. My priorities were wrapped up in the acceptance of others rather than God Himself.

The pain that I had numbed from the breakup finally hit me. My body would suddenly weaken, and uncontrollable sobs would drench my face. I was angry-angry for not protecting myself and allowing myself to endure through toxicity for so long. It was the fact of the abuse, the manipulation and mistreatment that I had not recognized that made my heart seethe in anger.

However, a point came when I remembered the note given to me at the conference, reminding me to thank God for what His love was willing to get me out of. God loved me so much to remove me from the situation. The truth was my constant pick-me-up. I would pray the small reminder over myself whenever emotions of regret and pain would seep in.

Eventually, as time went on, I learned a part of forgiveness is forgiving *myself* for enduring the mess I did. Though I forgave myself, I didn't give myself the time to sort through the effects of the relationship. Instead I hid away the painful feelings and continued my season.

Still, through the tears of heartbreak and praying the prayers the Lord prompted me to. I still hadn't received the fullness of what I needed to receive in the season I was in. The Lord placed a burning desire in my heart to be alone, after ignoring it for months, I isolated myself.

Though I finally had the time and solitude I needed to seek the Lord, I was still in a distracted place. I was focused on what I thought my last semester of college would look like, and was obsessed with how I'd make an appearance to my first semester at my university as a single woman. I wasn't looking for a man, but I wanted to be finally seen as *me*, rather than be seen as someone's shadow. Still, every plan I made didn't sit right with me. I had no peace doing anything *but* seeking the Lord.

One of the friends who prayed with me months earlier stopped speaking to me during the first week of school. Though I was confused as to what the issue was, I was inclined to leave it alone. I prayed, asking the Lord what was going on, and felt it placed on my heart that our friendship was coming to an end. Hearing this, I had a great amount of peace.

After a few days of us not speaking, she texted me to meet her so we could finally discuss the reason for the silence. When I did, she began to speak life into me. She heard the Lord's voice very clearly, and for the few months of our friendship, she was my source of hearing Him as well. However, that season had come and gone, and now the Lord desired to speak directly to me.

In our conversation, the Lord spoke through her, explaining this season would essentially be one of solitude in order for me to properly learn and develop a relationship with the Lord. She had been a distraction from me entering into this new season, and we both recognized it. I was grateful; by way of the Holy Spirit, she graciously let go of the friendship so I may begin to know the fullness of who I am. I couldn't have been more understanding of it. This idea of isolation was not new, as it had already been instructed to be by the voice of Jesus months prior. However, I had forfeited my season because I placed my convictions in the palm of another's comfort, and neglected the voice of God telling me to isolate myself.

The truth of the revelation refreshed and excited me. My spirit had been waiting for this. As the conversation continued, I agreed with her: it was time for us to part ways. I would no longer live my life in her shadow, or the shadow of anyone else for that matter, but rather begin to walk in the light. Hiding behind another's shadow was something I'd done for the majority of my life, as I'd always been afraid of what people would think of me. I quieted myself and let others have their show, with me only making an appearance as an extra in the background.

Despite my fears, the Lord had said He had other plans for me. However, before I could reintroduce myself as the main character behind God alone, I had to first be introduced to the real me and develop an authentic relationship with the Lord.

From there, my friend and I parted ways, our connection completely diminished. The door closed on everything that lived in the last season.

I left, excited to begin this new season. My desire was to know God. I had limited knowledge of Him, and the little I did know hadn't induced the powerful change in me I sought. It felt very surface-level, but I knew with everything in me: there was more to the Lord, and there was even more to myself. I couldn't deny it, and I made it my goal to discover the depth of Him, His love for me, and what my identity in Him truly was.

However, it was the epitome of "easier said than done." Walking into the season, I had assumed the process would last maybe a month, but to my surprise, I remained isolated for the entire semester. I had much to learn, much to heal from, and much to do. And so, on a warm September evening, my wilderness season began.

I kept a journal on me to keep track of my revelations, and to write down what I studied in the Word. I filled them up rather quickly, but I still consider each one to be my prized possessions. In those pages, I discovered myself and discovered God.

This was not my first time keeping journals. I had *always* written in journals. I wrote poems, my feelings, goals, and the things I studied in my quiet time. But, the dynamic of my old journals differed from the new. My old journals reeked of sadness, anxiety, and fear. I wrote from a place of brokenness. I cried for help with every ink-filled page.

As I reread what I had written only a year prior, I was in shock. I didn't realize I'd grown so much. I didn't realize I was so *broken* then. Still, I found the beauty resonating from those old journals. The beautiful thing was, I didn't recognize the author of the words which were so painfully written.

I was a new woman. I was more than I ever thought I'd be, all within a matter of a year. It gave me a push to seek the Lord even harder – I wanted to experience spiritual, mental, emotional, and physical growth in each season. I just wanted to *grow*.

As the season began, I was without a plan. I, for the most part, just did what I thought would be right. However, despite my best efforts, I lacked structure and discipline, which always resulted in my shortcomings.

After about two weeks, I grew frustrated. I felt as though I wasn't hearing from God, or feeling His presence. I didn't understand what I was doing wrong. I prayed, read my Word, and tried to be faithful in the things He had instructed me to be.

One night, as I pondered as to why I was not measuring up to my own standards, I made the decision to fast. I wrote a list of things I wanted to gain from this fast. I was expectant, but my optimism only last two days. I had no specifications of the type of fast I'd be doing. In those two days, however, I discovered my weakness: I was a complete slave to my flesh. I nearly cried of hunger waiting for the clock to strike 6pm, which was the time I decided I would eat. I hated every second of my fast, but hated my flesh had power over me even more.

I remember laying on the couch and hearing the Lord's voice say that He will teach me how to fast. I wanted to quit until I gained more knowledge on fasting, but evidently, the Lord wanted my own experience to give me the knowledge I needed.

The second day, I didn't struggle so much with hunger, but social media consumed me. I found myself scrolling aimlessly for hours. I felt as though I needed to log off, but I was sucked in. The longer I scrolled, the more useless my fast became. It began to lose its meaning; at this point, I was simply starving myself just for the sake of it. The reality of the thought frustrated me back into a place of seeking.

I began to pray according to the ways I had learnt from the book I was reading *Kingdom Prayer* by Tony Evans. I prayed specifically and accordingly to the scriptures. I was reminding the Lord of what He had spoken, and expected an answer. As I prayed without letting my mind wander, I heard the voice of the Lord telling me the hope of His calling. *To preach.* I shelved the thought of what He had spoken but thought if this truly *was* God, I needed confirmation.

During the next few days, I grew frustrated once again and asked the Lord what I was doing wrong. I wanted His attention and felt as though I couldn't grasp it. I felt disheartened but I refused to be defeated. If I needed to push a little harder, then it would be what I'd do.

Fasting was the only thing I lacked in my season of seeking, Determined, I planned to do the Daniel Fast for 21 days. I made a shopping list, and planned to wake up early to have devotion before my classes started. I found scriptures which supported my plan, and internally vowed to stick to it. I wanted to emulate Jesus in Mark 1:35.

"Very early in the morning, while it was still dark, Jesus got up, left the house and went off to a solitary place, where he prayed."

So, I set my alarm for 7am. I woke up the next morning with a reminder on my phone to join a prayer call with other women around the world. I had never done so before, but felt prompted to do so. I tiredly dialed the number and was immediately hit with revelation from the Lord. Before the prayer began, the woman first encouraged listeners with whatever the Lord had placed on her heart.

I scurried for my journal and a pen so I may encourage myself with these reminders throughout my season. It was a warning to be aware of how the enemy didn't want me to win, and despite his efforts, I was close to it – close to victory, close to becoming who God wanted me to be.

I was close, but I had to remain persistent. She brought up the story of Daniel, declaring how he didn't stop praying, and neither should we. Even if we experience attack, we must stand immovable, remain in position, and submit to God. She said something I continue to hear to this day: lives depend on me fulfilling the assignment placed over my life.

As the call was coming to an end, she prayed this: "May this week be a week of clarity and confirmation for you. Not only will you receive answers, but the strategy to follow through." It became my prayer for the rest of the day.

I leapt out of bed after the call and began to do some interceding of my own. I attempted to get in the Word, but was so scattered, I only received bits and pieces from multiple books. However, looking back, I believe the call alone was everything the Lord could reveal to me in my quiet time. Shortly after that I was dressed and out the door for class.

I returned home and relaxed. My idea of unwinding at this time was watching a sermon or two. Afterwards, I decided to go on a walk. As I walked, I prayed silently to myself, staring at the setting sky. I wrote a small prayer in my notes, gushing out my desires to the Lord. As I did, He filled my empty spaces with clarity and strategy. My prayer was this –

Father God, there is more to you Lord, more to who you created me to be. I pray this week is one of clarity and strategy. Teach me to maximize this season, Lord, with daily, consistent, and persistent devotion and praying according to the scripture. I know these practices are vital and should not be stopped even after this season ends. I need to find scripture for every area of my life, Lord. I ask your

Holy Spirit to lead me to them. I really want to know you more and more intimately. To have an immovable relationship with you. I want to be obedient and be like a sheep who knows your voice. I want to be like Abraham, who you called your friend. I want to be like Elijah, who was persistent in prayer. You have equipped me for those things, God. Open my spiritual eyes to truly see that. I want to be sensitive to your Holy Spirit. Amen.

Once I returned home, I wrote down everything the Lord had told me. He told me to be persistent and strategic in devotion and to know exactly what I would be reading every day, even if it meant planning the night before. This essentially prompted me to develop a reading plan and to have an inductive Bible study of some sort to help me further understand the Word. I used Bible studies I found on Grace-Bible.org. Using them prevented me from aimlessly reading chapter after chapter, without gaining deeper knowledge or acquiring personal revelation. I was instructed to pray and write specific, scripture-filled prayers for every area of my life, focusing on things I had been really struggling to overcome. That same night I constructed a reading plan, following the one I found on Grace-Bible.org. I initially wanted to begin in Romans but the Lord kept pressing Ephesians on my heart. In this book, my journey of discovering the Lord began.

The following morning, I arose early. I created an atmosphere conducive for meeting the Lord, one where I wouldn't be tempted to fall back asleep. This was a meeting with God I had orchestrated, one I deemed of high importance and one I refused to miss. I freshened up, gathered my necessary belongings from my room, and settled in the dining room. I adjusted myself to face the window, through which I could see the extraordinary sunrise peeking through the blinds. I breathed in the presence of the Lord as I lit a candle, filling my tiny apartment with the aroma of relaxing scents.

On my dining room table, I arranged my notebook, Bible, laptop, and writing utensils and began my study. I repeated these steps daily, no matter what. I forced myself out of bed some days, and every day I did I was proud of myself. I grew in love with this routine. It was time with a Father I desperately wanted to know.

As I discovered the depth of Him, He began to reveal to me the hope of who He called me to be: His daughter. He began to show me truths I sought for in man. Truths which healed me. Truths which sustained me. Truths which I didn't think applied to me.

As I read Ephesians, these truths began to manifest in my heart. I used these scriptures to affirm my identity in Christ, the main being - I am loved. Even while I was in my mess, I was *loved.* Even when the Lord knew the routes I would take, He loved *me.* Many days, I cried at the dining room table, soaking in the presence of the Lord. Eventually, I added worship to the mix. I'd sing to the Lord with tears staining my cheeks, but feeling freedom rise in my chest. His love had me swooning.

After my first study, I wrote on my white board: I am predestined, I am chosen, and I am loved. I recited these things out loud often until they were etched permanently in my heart. This truth excited me. I loved the *love* behind Ephesians, but even more than that, I loved this was the first book God wanted me to read. It was as though before all else, He wanted to remind me of the love He has always had for me.

The second day, He prompted me to do a full fast – no food till 6 pm. I noticed my flesh had constantly wanted to be gratified, and typically, I would quickly satisfy the desire. When I didn't, my thoughts would be overwhelmed with the things my flesh wanted. But, in my moment of wanting to wave the white flag to fasting, I realized something. If I could not abstain from food without anticipating my next meal - how then, would I ever be able to fully abstain from a man? In almost everything, I gave myself what I wanted, but if I couldn't resist food for less than 24 hours, I would seriously question my ability to merely have the desire to wait to have sex until marriage. I recognized dwelling on a thing is nearly as bad as doing a thing. To dwell on my flesh is to be led by my flesh. If something so simple as food caused me to dwell so deeply on my flesh, wouldn't having a man in my life provoke the same thing?

Being that lust had already been a struggle in my past, I knew I needed to take every thought captive, no matter how minute they may have seemed. Even towards food. I needed fasting to teach me to resist my flesh. I was exhausted, my body ached, and I wanted nothing more than some junk food. Nonetheless, I pressed through, and did so weekly. It was every Tuesday, in the midst of my Daniel Fast, when I denied myself food. Rather than thinking about when I would eat next, I changed my mindset to how much more I could get of God in the time period of me not eating.

As I continued my study, the Lord was still revealing to me the power of prayer. As I read Ephesians, I recognized how Paul explained in one verse the things the Lord had promised for us, as believers. Then, in another verse, he prays for those same things.

I was intrigued. If it were promised, why did I need to pray? Of course, I needed to fight in prayer for the things which are mine, but there was more to it. Though my prayer life had grown, there was still a lot for me to learn.

I found praying for the things which have already been promised pulls down the hand of God. Persistent prayer moves Him, and when He is reminded of His word, they do no return void (Isaiah 55:11). Meaning, He is faithful to fulfill them, which also was why I needed to pray according to the scriptures.

It was becoming a full circle. However, my prayers could not be limited to only myself and what the Lord had promised me. I had to begin extending my prayers to cover those in my life as well. It was the will of God. It's what Jesus meant when He said to pray like this in the Lord's prayer, and say, "Thy will be done." His will is for all people to come into the knowledge of who He is and receive salvation. This was something Paul stressed and constantly did himself.

So, I began to do the same. My prayer life changed as I began to incorporate so many vital things. First, I praised the name of Jesus, exalting Him and simply who He is. Then, I covered others and their needs in prayer and brought myself, and my requests to His feet last. I ended every prayer with praising Him in advance of His blessings, and gave Him the praise, honor, and glory. This, of course, took more time. I found my prayer time gradually increase, but it was because I abandoned the shallow habitual prayer and began to yield to the spirit, allowing God to take me deeper than I had ever been before.

Eventually, after much prompting from the Spirit, I finally wrote out my scripture-filled prayers. I had one over my thoughts, my day, my sleep, my discernment, one I would pray when fear crept in, and when the enemy tried to remind me of my past. I even had one I prayed when I had no desire to pray. I prayed these daily. I plastered them on my wall, I saved them to my laptop and phone. Everywhere I went, I had them. They were my holy grail. They were starting points in my prayer; I would recite them as written, then flow into wherever else the spirit of God would lead me. I was determined to solidify my prayer life, even if it came by forcing my flesh.

As the 21 days of my fast progressed and I fell deeper into love with the Lord, He exposed the depth of His love for me. The most significant revelations he gave me came from a memory during my freshman year in college. I sat outside our school's cafeteria as I spoke to my now ex-boyfriend. Before he and I began a relationship, I explained to him that I was not one he could simply *have*. I wanted to be *pursued* by a man of God. I said those things wanting them to be true, but they ultimately held no weight because of the countless times I had carelessly given myself to him.

Now, I sat in the middle of my bedroom, still wanting the same pursuit from a man someday. But the Lord quickly corrected me concerning my desires of a man. You see, the more I read, prayed, and worshipped, the Lord began to pour this revelation over me.

He was the first to pursue me, even when I ignored Him and resisted Him. Even when I wanted to live in my filth, He pursued me. Likewise, I had always wanted a man to tell me I was beautiful and one who was capable of providing for me. However, God was the one who desired to do these things the most. He wanted me to see myself in His image, and He wanted me to know the depth of Him being Jehovah Jireh, God my provider.

I realized He is the greatest love I could ever have. He sees me according to His word. Fearfully and wonderfully made (Psalm 139:14), His handiwork, His workmanship (Ephesians 2:10), altogether beautiful and flawless (Songs 4:7) and radiant because of the way I looked upon Him. (Psalm 34:5). These were the truths He had always wanted me to hear and believe.

Yet, instead of finding the source which would constantly shower these truths on me, I ignorantly sought them out in man, leading me to more brokenness and disappointment.

But God wanted to change that. He wanted to be my first love. He wanted to set the standard. He wanted me to seek Him as the creator, rather than seeking the creation to affirm me, provide for me, and pursue me. He alone has and always will be the creator of those things. In Him alone will I ever find them.

I cried as these revelations rained down on me and I ended the night by worshipping. Here is when I began to slowly grasp the Lord's love for me. Experiencing His love had always been a difficult task for me to take hold of. I worked for it, even though it could not be earned. When I would fail to measure up to a ridiculously high standard I had placed upon myself, I would break down in tears, feeling as if I let the God of the universe down. But in these moments of seeking Him, He showed me how His love for me has always been eternal and constant. It has been unwavering, and though it disciplined me when I veered wrong, not even a cubic of it was stripped away from me.

I found He was the best love.

CHAPTER SEVENTEEN

A River in the Desert

*A*s my wilderness season continued, things began to shift. I spent countless mornings in tears because of the flaws and brokenness the Lord showed me I was dealing with. The biggest of these flaws was my need for the approval of people.

When the Lord revealed this to me, I was in disbelief. I found myself finally getting the thing I longed for – the voice of the Lord – and then disobeying it, because His instructions would affect my relationship with someone else. It was impossible for me to serve Him and please others as well. Something had to give.

He showed me this fault not to condemn me, but to heal me. As He revealed those things to me, He began the process of healing me as well. Each step was strenuous, and I cried often, as though I wouldn't make it. When my faith had gotten weak one morning, He reminded me He is faithful to bring a good work that He began to completion (Philippians 1:6). I believed Him; I had asked for a verse to sustain me for the rest of the season - this was it. I knew who I was on this particular day wouldn't be who I'd be in the long run, and because of this, I continued to push and seek the Lord.

I kept myself encouraged every day with Deuteronomy 8, which described the purpose of my wilderness season. The Lord would remind me of this daily –

"Remember, the Lord your God led you on the entire journey through these 40 years in the wilderness, so that He might humble you and test you to know what was in your heart, whether or not you would keep His commands. He humbled you by letting you go hungry; then he gave you manna to eat, which you have and your fathers have not known, so that you might learn that man does not live on bread alone but on every word that comes from the mouth of God."

Reading this entire passage every morning, I knew this season was not in vain. I knew there was a purpose and an end result I desperately needed to gain. It was the length of the season that drained me. I stood still at the beginning, peering to see the finish line. Not even a blur would appear in my vision, and it exhausted me. I loved the Lord, but I wanted to go out and put my faith to the test, and continue to cultivate relationships. But it simply wasn't the time.

While it was sometimes daunting and often excruciatingly long, I found solace in coming home to be engulfed in the presence of God. Despite the weakness of my flesh, my spirit was on fire.

In that season, I learned so much. He gave me a partial sneak peek of the blueprints to who He wanted me to be, and it was the most revitalizing thing I have ever experienced. I saw myself in places I never would have imagined, doing things I would never do by my own strength. But, it was what God saw fit me for me. Though it was too large for me to accomplish on my own, God wanted me to do these things so He may get the glory. Despite my insecurities, God had to remind me that my assignment was not about me, rather, it was about those who needed the saving grace of God.

I began to meet new people and develop friendships which aligned with who I was becoming. They motivated and pushed me, and many of them were encouragingly in the same type of season as me. They became vital in my growth, confirmed things the Lord had for me, and related to me and understood my season in ways I truly needed. Seeing their relationship with the Lord, as well as what I gained from studying scripture, I began to ask myself questions like, "is my life lined up with the things I talk about?" I wondered if people could tell I was a Christian by my fruits. I asked God and myself how I could do better. I was beginning to feel a moment of full circle, as if I was seeing my identity fall into place as my love for God and my desire to follow Him increased.

As I felt as though I was at my peak, my world stopped. My mother called me and told me that she found a large lump in her breast.

I lost my breath – I didn't understand, and cried. I called one of my close friends, and he prayed over her for healing and peace for me. I weakly got out of bed and began to intercede over her healing.

I cried out to God and rebuked the hand of the enemy over my family all at once. I was distraught, but tried to hold my faith intact, believing she would be okay. For years, my family and I had no insurance. But, by the faithfulness of the Lord, a couple who hired my parents put them, my brothers and I on their insurance plan to receive medical attention. This was not asked for, but was provided by no other than the Lord.

She was able to immediately go to the doctor's office to find the lumps were benign and could be removed. However, the process of getting there was painful.

I drove, missing classes, just so I could be at her doctor's appointments. I cried privately, and though my heart felt heavy, I remained constant in my prayer. I watched as tears would come to her eyes; all she wanted to come from her diagnosis was for her family to become closer.

Yet, I give glory to God for her test came back non-cancerous. Although my faith was tested, I learned how to prevail in prayer even with a broken heart.

My immediate family and I weren't very close – there was a lot of unspoken and undealt-with brokenness from all of us. I only spoke to some of my brothers, and didn't even know how the others were doing. We held onto anger and bitterness, but the Lord began to soften my heart and show me where I was at fault in the breaking. Wanting to see my family grow close, I wrote a prayer concerning them and prayed it daily. I eventually shared it with my parents, who made it their mission to pray it as well. We prayed this –

Father God, I lift my family up in your powerful name, and I pray according to Ezekiel 36:25-27. Lord, your word says you will sprinkle clean water on them so they may be cleaned. Cleanse them from all impurities and all idols. Give them a new heart and put a new spirit within them. Remove their hearts of stone and give them a heart of flesh. Place your spirit within them so they may follow your Word and observe your ordinances. I pray according to Acts 10:12, for all my family and I to become devout and God-fearing, generous to those in need, and for us to pray regularly. Lord, I pray in accordance to Colossians 3:13, that we forgive one another for any grievances we've caused, just as you've forgiven us. Lord make my family a unit! Allow us to draw near to you, Father God, and allow you to get all of the glory. Jesus, I love you and praise you for restoration in advance. Thank you, Lord. Amen.

As my mother got back on her feet emotionally and physically, my family got hit again with an attack which would cause months of testing. Seeing the stress my family endured, I took it upon myself to make sure my family had what they needed spiritually and emotionally. Doing so, however, came at a price.

I, as a graduating senior, lost all urgency for classes. I missed tests, failed assignments, and skipped lectures, all of which affected my grades. Those things, at the time, did not matter to me. I would have rather been home taking care of the needs of my family than getting done what needed to be done. While I believed I was graced, I also poured myself out significantly, draining myself.

One week, I felt an urgency to fast, and I did, so I might would see deliverance in my family. In the midst of the week, I was awakened out of my sleep by the spirit of the Lord, Psalms 81:6-7 ringing loudly in my spirit. I sleepily pulled out my phone and searched for the verse, jotted it down in my notes, and fell back asleep. The verse didn't significantly hit me until days to come.

At this point, I had fasted for about 4 days. I was certain - by my fasting, immediate deliverance would come. When the weekend came around, I drove down to my parents' house, prepared to pray away the issues my family was facing and to see chains fall to the ground.

But when I arrived, sadness rushed over me. Though I had planned to see change come in the house of my family, nothing, I could physically see, happened. Things were the same, and it overwhelmed me. I attempted to remain strong in the face of my family, not wanting to be a leak in the dam which made everyone else explode with emotion.

When I found an opportunity, I went to my car to cry. I couldn't bear seeing my family attacked in this way, and I felt useless to the cause. I let my pinned-up emotions rush out of me as I contemplated what I was doing wrong, and why I didn't see a change. In the midst of those thoughts, I recalled multiple friends with whom I disclosed the issue. I remembered them telling me to be still, and let God be God. I didn't understand what it meant. It felt passive. I didn't know what to do, or rather, what *not* to do. I felt paralyzed when thinking about the situation, so much so, I pushed aside my needs to tend to my family. I had not realized I was playing the role of God and expecting my actions alone to make a change, but I couldn't do it anymore. I was weak, and the weight of this burden was far too heavy for me to handle.

As my tears subsided, and after having a friend pray over me, the verse in Psalms came back to me. I read it again, aloud – "I relived his shoulders from the burden; his hands were freed from carrying the basket. You called out in distress, and I rescued you; I answered you from the thundercloud. I tested you at the waters of Meribah."

I read it again and cried in relief, finally understanding this was a battle I could not physically fight. The Lord, however, seeing me fight, took the gloves from my hands and reassured me of how He was in charge. My job was to continue to war in the spirit, but love in the natural. I couldn't and didn't need to overexert myself, which would leave me without a portion of strength. I was relieved upon the realization of how there was nothing I could physically do to speed up the process of what God was allowing. I had to trust the Lord had my family in His hands.

As I allowed God to be God, by removing my hands from manipulating the situation, I felt more joy and peace than I'd ever felt before. The Lord revealed to me my family would be healed and saved, and would sit in their right mind at His feet. This revelation alone made me drop to the floor in tears. I stopped physically fighting and allowed the power of prayer to become permeated on my lips. Though not immediately, I saw my family begin to shift, and are still shifting in the timing the Lord has ordained.

CHAPTER EIGHTEEN

A Walk to the End

*S*ince I lifted my hands in surrender to the Lord, I was able to find my rhythm with school again. Graduation was approaching quickly, and I still had assignments and finals that needed to be completed. I was able to pull my grades up after seeing them slip; I'd neglected my schoolwork when I put the weight of my family on my back. Even though I didn't complete a class in time, I was given permission to walk with outstanding credits, as long as I completed them within the next few months.

My cap and gown were a sleek black, and my dress was also black with small beaded stones covering the body of my dress.

I'd found my dress just days before graduation. When it was finally hanging in my closet next to the rest of my celebratory garments, anxiety lifted off of my shoulders. I had always been the type to love having my hair and nails done, so I made arrangements just 48 hours before graduation so everything could still be fresh. I chose long, red diamond-encrusted stiletto nails to accent my dress and complement my tassel, and long, pin straight black hair to top off the look.

Things were coming together, but the night before graduation, I had a breakdown. I was alone, as I had been for the entirety of the semester. The friends I had made weren't available, and the ones who were, I'd convinced myself wouldn't want to be around me while I broke down on the floor of my apartment. I wanted my family to be with me right then, and though we spent most of the night on FaceTime, they wouldn't be able to arrive until the day of graduation. Out of obedience, the man who had my heart and I weren't speaking. This left me with no one. My tears weren't solely based off of the fact I was alone. Rather, they were a result of the reality of me graduating.

I was scared. I was afraid of what was next. I knew I hadn't gone through a season of preparation for no reason. There was something bigger than me going to come into my life, and I knew it – *I felt it.*

I'm not sure why I spent the night alone, but as I did, a million thoughts captivated me. Perhaps it was my time to reflect, or my time to praise the Lord for bringing me out alive, but whatever the reason, all I felt was anxiety rise in my bones and a nervousness settle over me. All I kept thinking was how tomorrow, at graduation, I would begin the rest of my life.

I doubted my readiness. I had become used to routine, I was comfortable in college, and wanted to stay longer so I wouldn't be flung into my purpose. I wanted to prolong this season, but despite how I felt, I knew it was my time to walk. Despite my own feelings, my life had begun, and while it would be different, this would be a newness I would walk in with my head held high.

I felt this assurance as I walked across the stage at graduation. I would be closing a book to an awfully long story, and begin the sequel of walking in restoration. I cried until I drifted off to sleep, awaiting for the sun to shine on my face and dry my tears, as I prepared to turn the final page.

On December 15, 2018, I would become the first Mitchell to ever complete college. Neither of my parents had finished, and my brothers all took different, but successful, avenues. But for me, I would be receiving a degree in psychology. This degree saved me mentally and provided professors who pushed me spiritually.

But truthfully, it wasn't about the degree. For me, it was about the experience. It was about the pain and restoration I had gone through in a three-and-a-half-year time period. I had begun this journey fearfully bound, but left free and loved.

My college experience was unlike most. They were the years I discovered the Lord, and began to see the depth of who I was created to be. I sat in isolation for a total of three-and-a-half months, fasting, praying, and discovering. I received the fullness of what I could be in college because of those three months of submission. I received freedom. I felt chains break and a newness arise from me. I found how in Christ, I was a new creation. I became a new woman in those three months, one who I would have looked up to and adored in my younger years.

I became *me. Restored.*

My broken pieces were put back together, and I became better than what I was before. College saved me. Finding Christ in college saved me, all because I was obedient in those ten days when God prepared me to leave my ex. This event alone foundationally built the essence of who I am today. It was in the midst of my fasting and praying when all the weight which had built up over the course of almost two decades fell from me in less than a year. God shifted my heart from a person who once wore a hard exterior built of insecurities and fear, to a person who longs to see through His eyes, to practice love, and to walk in joy. My heart has been softened, revealing the compassion it holds. My mouth has been washed out, leaving only the desire to speak edifying words. I realized I wasn't who I thought I was, all those times when I came up drained and felt the need to force a conversation with the Lord. Now, I feel natural and light.

As if being washed of all impurities and getting dressed in silk, I walked carefully, watching my step, but trusting my feet will land in victory.

It's an ongoing beautiful process, seeing the evolution of me. First, I had to take the time and sit with myself in stillness and truth to recognize the characteristics placed within, which God entrusted in me. He knew they wouldn't be misused when discovered. I can't pretend to be who I am not, because God sees through the act. Blessed are those who are themselves, not whom they pretend to be. I had to realize my "I am" statements, and walk in them daily.

I am compassionate.

I am powerful.

I am fearless. God was faithful to me in my moments of faithfulness. He is still increasingly faithful to me, and He is desiring to reveal his faithfulness to *you*.

With these things in mind, I crossed the graduation stage, received my degree, and ended an awfully long book.

Acknowledgements

The support of the people who have been so graciously placed into my life has sustained my motivation to bring this book into its completion. Without the ones whom share a home in my heart I would not have had the extra push needed to begin the fulfillment of my God-given purpose. The Word is true when it advises that two are better than one (Ecclesiastes 4:9-12). With that being said, thank you to a few of my closest friends. Jaiáhn, who has scarified her time to offer incensed filled prayers on my behalf. The women who I not only call friend but my sister. Thank you. To the man that has given me hope to love, you inspire me daily because of the joy that exudes through you. You are so much to me, but in all you are my friend. Lastly, my mother, a women full of strength and beauty, a woman who is more impactful that I will ever be. Thank you for passing the torch to embark on this journey. You ma'am inspire me and to walk out the calling the Lord has placed over my life. I love you.
I love you all.

To all of those who have also been a voice of love to me. I appreciate you beyond measure. Your words, obedience, and simple presence in my life has made my process of healing and restoration doable.

Lastly, to you who have read my story. Thank you – you are forever in my prayers and my love for you is unreal. Thank you for the support and for choosing to *heal.*

www.ingramcontent.com/pod-product-compliance
Lightning Source LLC
LaVergne TN
LVHW041324080426
835513LV00008B/587